~A~
Field Guide
to Lucid
Dreaming

MASTERING THE ART *of*
ONEIRONAUTICS

~A~

Field Guide
to Lucid
Dreaming

A
Field Guide
to Lucid
Dreaming

MASTERING THE ART *of*
ONEIRONAUTICS

Dylan Tuccillo, Jared Zeizel, and Thomas Peisel
with illustrations by Mahendra Singh

WORKMAN PUBLISHING, NEW YORK

Library of Congress Cataloging-in-Publication Data

Tuccillo, Dylan.
  A field guide to lucid dreaming : mastering the art of oneironautics / by Dylan Tuccillo, Jared Zeizel, and Thomas Peisel ; with illustrations by Mahendra Singh.
      pages cm
  Includes bibliographical references.
  ISBN 978-0-7611-7739-5 (alk. paper)
1. Lucid dreams. I. Title.
  BF1099.L82T83 2013
  154.6'3--dc23   2013009227

Workman Publishing Company, Inc.
225 Varick Street
New York, NY 10014-4381
workman.com

WORKMAN is a registered trademark of Workman Publishing Co., Inc.

Printed in the United States of America
First printing August 2013

10 9 8 7 6 5 4 3 2

CONTENTS

FOREWORD

We shall not cease from exploration
And the end of all our exploring
Will be to arrive where we started
And know the place for the first time.

—T. S. Eliot,
POET, PLAYWRIGHT, AKA "OLD POSSUM"

For as long as there have been blank spots on the map, there have been pioneers—those unafraid of the fringe, who relish the untamed, the unknown, and the undiscovered. These individuals are inspired by the adventurous impulse to survey new ground, to chart new territory, or to discover new ideas. They are the innovators, creators, visionaries, and explorers.

Today we find ourselves on the brink of yet another frontier. You, holding this book, are about to enter this unknown world. Where are you going? What's left that hasn't already been mapped out? The only blank spots left are in the depths of the sea and in the vastness of outer space, but you won't be going to either of these places. This journey is a tad different. You won't find this place on any map.

You're not a stranger to this land. In fact you've traveled there every night of your life, whether you realize it or not. You leave your familiar world and experience this place, which has its own rules, customs, laws, and native population. You can traverse this frontier just like you'd walk through a forest. Here, you can learn, discover, heal, and awaken to different realities.

If you've read the cover of this book, you know what we're getting at: dreams! The goal of this book is to help you explore your dreams using the art of lucid dreaming. We will explain what lucid dreaming is and how you too can use it to survey the ground floor of your own subconscious. We will teach you how to become an *oneironaut,* a word derived from Greek that means "dream navigator."

Lucid dreaming is the ability to know you're dreaming while you're dreaming. A lucid dreamer is able to go to sleep at night and wake up within his or her dream. With this unique awareness, you can generally behave like someone who is awake, exercising the free will, imagination, and memory of waking life. Once lucid, you can explore and even change elements of the dream.

If you were to travel down the Amazon River, you'd need a field guide to tell you which plants to eat, how to navigate the terrain, and what to do when dealing with the natives. Consider this book your field guide to the dream world, a map to navigate through your subconscious. If you're a newcomer to lucid dreaming, the idea of exploring your subconscious may seem crazy or daunting. Don't you worry, we searched for the best techniques out there, made some improvements, and then boiled them down to their simplest forms. For those of you who have already experienced lucid dreaming, this guide will help you master this ability while traveling beyond what you thought was possible.

We'll teach you:

1. How to reconnect with your dreams

2. How to have a lucid dream

3. What to do once you're lucid

This book is filled with step-by-step advice, stories from the dream world, and wonderfully maddening ideas. It's based on our own experiences with a decade of lucid dreaming as well as the real-life experiences of many other lucid dreamers, writers, and scientists. Our goal was to report back from the dream world and write about the things that we actually observed and experienced.

Unlike other field guides, this book is designed to be read from start to finish, just as if you were to travel down a jungle trail. Information from the first chapter will be used in the second chapter; tips from the second chapter will pop up in the third chapter, and so on. So try and hold off the urge to jump around.

Here's an important note to remember before embarking on this inner journey: While dreaming is a skill that can improve with practice and focus, it's not something foreign to you. You dream. You do so every single night, whether you remember it or not.

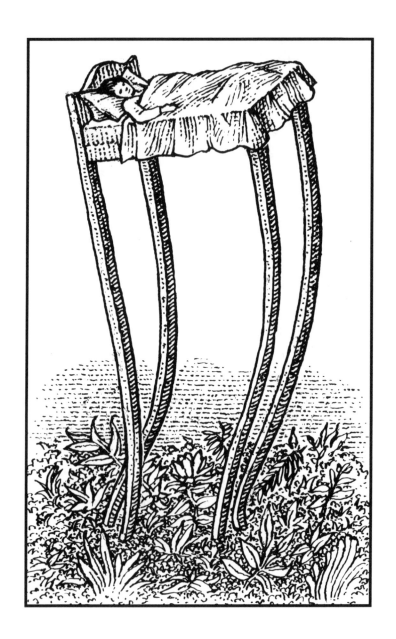

Ready to start? Here's your first lesson. The icon of a compass, seen above, will appear many times throughout this book. **TRY THIS**: Every time you see a compass, ask yourself the question "Am I dreaming at this very moment?" Look around you and really try to answer this question.

It may sound ridiculous to doubt your reality (of course you're awake, after all, you're reading this book). But for reasons you will soon learn, this reality check is the first step in waking up in your dreams. If you're able to master this technique, you'll have no problem with lucid dreaming.

So take a moment now and ask yourself this seemingly bizarre question:

"Am I dreaming?"

PART ONE

STARTING

the

JOURNEY

1

A New Discovery

It's April 12, 1975, in the Department of Psychology at the University of Hull in England. Researcher Keith Hearne is trying desperately to stay awake. He sits alone, monitoring a man named Alan Worsley as he sleeps, watching the monotonous up-and-down charting of ink on his polysomnograph machine. Worsley looks the same as any sleeper does—eyes closed, chest rising and falling. It's almost 8:00 a.m., and so far there is nothing out of the ordinary about this quiet Saturday morning. But in just a few minutes something incredible will occur.

At this very moment, these two scientists are attempting to make a discovery that will change history. They are trying to prove scientifically an esoteric ability that humans have known about for centuries: We can be consciously awake inside our dreams.

An obvious obstacle stands in the way of this would-be breakthrough: How can such a strange and ridiculous claim be proven? Worsley has experienced plenty of lucid dreams before. It won't be hard for him to become conscious inside of his own dream. But how does he prove that he's lucid? It's not as if Worsley can bring a camera into the dream world and bring back some Polaroids. To prove such an ability, our researchers will need a way to communicate from the dream world back to the waking world. They need some sort of phone line, a way for Worsley to "call" Hearne and tell him he's dreaming.

Since this feat has never been pulled off by modern science, these two men cannot rely on past experiments to figure out how to do it.

They are all alone, navigating the uncharted fringes of science. Luckily, Hearne and Worsley have an idea.

A few basic scientific facts helped develop their clever theory. You see, while our minds are active during a dream, our physical bodies are turned off. The body is essentially paralyzed when we venture off to the Land of Nod; the motor neurons in our brains are not stimulated, and the body's muscles are dormant. This is a normal state known as sleep atonia. Fortunately there are two parts of the body that remain unaffected by the paralysis: the diaphragm, so we can keep breathing, and the eyes. Our hotshot scientists came into the lab that day with a hypothesis: If Worsley moved his eyes back and forth inside the dream world, the physical eyes of his sleeping body would echo the same pattern of eye movement. The eyes would be the phone line, a way to communicate between these two worlds.

In the dream I entered my house at night. I flipped the switch to turn on the kitchen lights. The lights did not come on (a common problem in my dreams). It caused me to ask whether I was dreaming or not, which I knew the answer to immediately. I proceeded into the house now fully aware that I was dreaming. I saw my brother. I remembered that my objective tonight was to interact more with dream characters. —RICHARD V. W.

I'm in a high-rise apartment building with glass windows. A villain taunts me outside. He's flying on some sort of skateboard device. Realizing the absurdity of the situation I realize that I'm dreaming. "I'm dreaming!" I think to myself and I jump out of the building wearing nothing but swimming shorts. I fly toward him, trying to catch up. He is much faster than I am, but I'm able to mirror his movements and keep up with him. We chase each other, weaving around and in between buildings. I can read his subtle movements like we're two birds chasing after each other. I put my head down and fly in a straight line no longer following his lead. I grab ahold of him! Holding the back of his flying device I fling him high into the air. Not sure what happens to him after that. I wake up. —MIGUEL H.

At 8:07 a.m., Worsley finds himself in a dream, aware that he is dreaming and that his physical body is lying unconscious in the waking world. He then carries out specific, agreed-upon eye patterns—left to right eight times—in order to signal to the lab that he is in fact dreaming and doing so consciously. "The signals were coming from another world—the world of dreams," wrote Hearne, "and they were as exciting as if they were coming from another solar system in space." The EEG readout confirmed it, charting Worsley's brain activity: He was physically asleep, yet he was aware enough to signal back to the laboratory. He was lucid dreaming.

Three years later, a man named Stephen LaBerge would conduct a similar test at Stanford University. Without any knowledge of Hearne's experiments, LaBerge completed his doctoral dissertation, trying to prove the same thing: Conscious dreaming was not hogwash, but an actual, provable experience. Using the same eye-signaling technique, he too was successful. More tests were done to confirm the findings, and the news spread. There was now scientific proof of what the ancients had been telling us for centuries.

We can be awake in our dreams.

Becoming Aware

Before we talk about the fine subtleties of dream adventures, let's take a step back and ask the obvious question: What exactly is a lucid dream? A lucid dream is one in which you become aware that you're dreaming. Not to be confused with a very vivid dream, a lucid dream is the present-moment realization that you're dreaming, a sudden self-reflective epiphany of, "Wait a second . . . I'm dreaming!" You may notice that you're in a location that would normally be impossible (Wait, how did I get to Hawaii?) or perhaps you stumble upon something absolutely absurd (Is that an ostrich driving a car?). Maybe your trigger has more to do with

O-NEIR-O-NAUT-ICS

Oneironaut is derived from two Greek words, oneira meaning "dreams" and nautis meaning "sailor." An oneironaut is someone who has learned to travel consciously in the dream world, exploring its terrain with a high degree of clarity and awareness.

Getting out of bed and standing on my feet, I performed a reality check by looking at my digital watch, looking away, and looking back at it again. As the digital numbers did change, I still wasn't entirely convinced that it was a dream because everything was so vivid and real. —BEN S.

> With regard to my early lucid dreams, the earliest I can remember were when I was just starting middle school (around twelve years old), and they would almost always start off with me being at school and walking around the hallways. Even though everything felt like it did in real life, I would eventually get a sense that something was off and that the world I was in might not be real. Eventually I developed a strategy to test whether or not I was actually dreaming; I would "find" a bathroom and look into the toilet. If I saw my reflection in the toilet I would know I was dreaming and then go about interacting with the dream fully aware. —WILL B.

your past (Wait a second, I'm not in college anymore! This has to be a dream!). Typically, lucid dreams are triggered by some sort of inconsistency, something that suddenly causes the dreamer to stop and question his or her reality.

Once you become lucid, you'll have complete memory of your waking life, and will be able to think logically, make decisions, and explore the dream's landscape in the same way you'd traverse the physical world. You'll have direct influence over the entire dream and its content. Whereas in a regular dream, you would react blindly, unable to reflect on your current situation, you now hold the reins—your mind is awake enough to call the shots. Have a conversation with a dream character, fly across a mountain range, breathe underwater, pass effortlessly through walls—these are just a few examples. No longer confined to a physical body, you have the freedom to travel over large distances, move at incredible speeds, or even transcend time as you know it.

When you realize that you are not separate from the inner world of your dreams, you can move, shape, even create objects out of thin air. Everything in the environment around you takes on a very intimate relationship; you might even say that the world around you is you! If it seems like we're exaggerating, we're not: The sensations of touch, smell, sight, taste, and sound will seem just as vivid as they do in waking life. If you've ever seen the sci-fi film *The Matrix,* you already have a good idea what this world is like: a place that seems real but is just a projection of the mind. As the character Morpheus describes The Matrix, "If real is what you can feel, smell, taste, and see, then 'real' is simply electrical signals interpreted by your brain." But unlike *The Matrix,* lucid dreaming is not science fiction.

Imagine being free of your physical body, leaving behind silly things like gravity. Picture yourself flying, and doing so in the literal sense, feeling the air rushing across your face, the weightlessness of your body, breaking every Newtonian law out there. Imagine seeing and conversing with the natives of the dream who provide valuable insights and knowledge about your life. Hidden in this place you can find wisdom and guidance that could change your life.

I find myself flying and realize that I must be in a dream. Now lucid, I slow my flying down and take in the scenery in front of me. I am overlooking the most beautiful sight I have ever seen. My vision seems to capture everything for miles. Grassy hills and evergreen trees line the ground below me. The sky. Oh, the sky! It is painted with the most incredible shades of pink and orange I have ever witnessed! The sun in the distance looks like it is setting, the clouds standing out in their vibrant hues. I am brought to tears from the sheer beauty of such a sight. I lie on my back in midflight and close my eyes—I wake up.
—RACHEL T.

Can Anyone Do It?

From an early age we're told we can do anything that we put our minds to. As we grow up, those reassuring words start to lose their credibility. Not everyone can keep a beat, and math doesn't come naturally to us all. Fortunately, anyone can have a lucid dream. The ability is not something you have to acquire, it's something you already possess. In fact, studies show that most of us can boast of having at least one lucid dream. In a 1998 study of one thousand average Austrians, 26 percent of participants reported having at least one lucid dream in their lifetime. When 439 German students were asked the same question, 82 percent of them had experienced a lucid dream and a whopping 10 percent reported experiencing a lucid dream two or three times a month! Without any training, these average citizens witnessed the completely natural state of a conscious dream. That same German study concluded that one's personality was not a major factor. Whether you are liberal, conservative, extroverted, or introverted, you can become lucid.

All that's really required to make the jump from normal dreaming into lucid dreaming is for you to recognize the dream state. This realization can happen spontaneously in any number of ways and can be induced with the help of some simple techniques.

You don't need anything to become lucid in your dreams. You don't need drugs or any special equipment to begin your pioneering journey—you already have all the necessary requirements: a decently intelligent brain, a spot of patience, and a few slivers of free time. This book will simply show you how to unlock a dormant potential.

Benefits of Lucid Dreaming

Never had I felt so absolutely well, so clear-brained, so divinely powerful,
so inexpressibly free! The sensation was exquisite beyond words;
but it lasted only a few moments, and I awoke.

—Oliver Fox,
writer, dream explorer of the early 20th century

L ucid dreaming is an experience beyond words. Attempts to describe it often fail, a pungent wedge of Gouda flattened down into a slice of American cheese. There are the exhilarating adventures of flying and superpowers. Then, after a few lucid dreams, many people experience a drastic alteration in their perspectives—they realize that there is much more to reality than what they currently understand. Some are no longer afraid of death! Many say that lucid dreams are the best experiences they've had in their lives.

1. Adventure and Fantasy

Indiana Jones, eat your heart out. Many people begin lucid dreaming because of the desire for adventure and the allure of doing the impossible. Flying and having sex seem to be the first activities of the novice lucid dreamer. Film director Michel Gondry told *The Guardian* that when he becomes lucid, "I generally end up having sex with the first girl I can find." Since physical laws and social boundaries don't exist in the dream world like they do here, lucidity provides the perfect playground for your fantasies to run free.

Leap up a giant mountain, run into some magical creatures, chat with a dead celebrity, shrink down a few sizes and see the world from an ant's perspective, or picnic on top of a locomotive steam train. Why not?

2. Facing Nightmares

For some people, nightmares are a real problem. Ambushed at night by their fears, many people avoid their nightmares by forgetting their dreams altogether, a kind of safety mechanism. But if you become lucid in a nightmare, you not only have the power to change the plot of the scary story of your subconscious, you have the power to heal and find the source of what's plaguing you. So seize this opportunity: Face your monsters and defuse your nightmares, rather than running away from them.

3. Creativity and Inspiration

Dreams are a creative person's wonderland. By becoming consciously aware in dreams, you'll be able to tap into incredible amounts of knowledge and inspiration. If you're writing a book, talk face-to-face with one of the main characters. Get Einstein to explain to you the theory of relativity, compose music, write a speech. If you believe that the dream world is created by your subconscious mind, then it is the ideal location to let your creativity run wild. Free of limitations, you can create pretty much anything you want.

4. Creative Problem Solving

Lucid dreams can be used as a testing ground, a way to try out new skills. Imagine giving that quarterly presentation to a room of people in your dreams first, where you feel in control and relaxed. If you play sports, imagine winning that upcoming race, scoring that goal, beating that record, before any of it happens in the physical world. Got a problem that needs solving? Look to your dream for advice. Asking dreams for guidance is an ancient practice and a great way to find insights into everyday problems.

5. Healing
Physical ailments can sometimes result from an emotional or spiritual imbalance. Dream healing has been around for millennia, beginning with the ancient Egyptians. Got an illness, a broken

Before going to bed I wanted to dream about boxing. I dreamed I was going to a boxing tournament in the projects, and when I got there they said there was no one for me to fight in my weight class. As I started to leave, I realized this was the dream that I had been wanting to have and it made me go lucid. I told someone to go find me a competitor and they came back with a guy I could fight. So we started boxing in the ring and it felt exactly like the real thing. I felt my lungs breathing, my heart rate up, my muscles when I punched, and it hurt when I took shots. I was also able to control the skill level of the guy I was fighting so he wasn't a pushover. It felt like I was training in real life. The only difference was that I wasn't actually sustaining a bloody nose, it just felt like it. —KYLE O.

> I was amazed at how realistic everything felt when I first learned how to become lucid in my dreams. Some of my first lucid dreams were spent just walking around feeling dream objects. I was blown away by the visceral feeling and tactile sensations. Things felt just like they did in the waking world! When I walked, I could feel the weight of my body, the brush of my clothes against my skin. When I touched something, I could feel its weight and texture, I could smell the aroma of a flower, or the heat of the sun. How could my mind be creating all of this?
> —THOMAS P.

bone, depression, a broken heart? In a lucid dream, you can heal many aspects of yourself. You can become happier and more whole.

6. Self-knowledge

Dreams often act like mirrors, presenting you with a "reflection" of yourself. By becoming conscious in your subconscious, you're able to explore and deepen the connection to your own inner world. Who are you? What do you want? Lucid dreaming can be a practical tool for soul-searching, a way of getting in touch with your deeper self.

The Road Ahead

Regarded as a mystical event during ancient times, lucid dreaming has left the occult circles and entered into the modern world. A 2007 *New York Times* article noted that "the esoteric practice, which has been acknowledged in the West since at least 1867, seems on the verge of becoming much better known." Lucid dreaming has been recognized by mainstream science and is popping up in films and TV shows, a real ability that anyone can learn and thousands already practice. For you, this means one thing: It has never been easier to learn how to lucid dream.

You may become aware in your dreams tonight. The experience might happen spontaneously or it might happen with the help of some techniques described in the chapters to come. It might take a day, a week, or perhaps a month. Regardless, by the end of this book, you'll know what it's like to be completely conscious inside your dreams. With a little help, you'll be blazing the trails of your dream's landscape, mastering the skills of creation, flight, incubation, and numerous other abilities.

What Are Dreams?

If the dream is a translation of waking life,
waking life is also a translation of the dream.

—René Magritte,
painter, lover of bowler hats and green apples

Each night, under the veil of sleep, with our eyes closed and the outside world shut out, a new world appears, familiar but different. Powerful, absurd, mysterious, frightening, beautiful, dangerous, realistic, baffling—it's nearly impossible to describe what dreams are or how they make us feel. Before you can become lucid in your dreams, you need to understand the nature of dreams. In this section we'll get to the heart of what dreams are as we ask: How much do we really know about them, anyway? Then, with your head screwed on tight, you'll begin your journey into the dream world.

A CREATIVE DREAMER

Paul McCartney woke up one morning with the tune of "Yesterday" playing in his head. "I liked the melody a lot," he said, "but because I'd dreamed it, I couldn't believe I'd written it. I thought, 'No, I've never written anything like this before.' But I had the tune, which was the most magical thing!" A dream was also an inspiration for another Beatles classic. McCartney describes the experience: "One night during this tense time I had a dream I saw my mum, who'd been dead ten years or so. And it was so great to see her because that's a wonderful thing about dreams: You actually are reunited with that person for a second; there they are and you appear to both be physically together again. It was so wonderful for me and she was very reassuring. In the dream she said, 'It'll be all right.' I'm not sure if she used the words 'Let it be' but that was the gist of her advice."

Dreams have fascinated us since the beginning of time. They have always been a part of humanity's story, guiding us in nearly every field of endeavor. They have been studied, worshipped, and practiced by nearly every culture throughout history.

In modern times, dreams have been responsible for at least two Nobel Prizes, incredible scientific breakthroughs, invaluable inventions, novels, works of art, and many other discoveries.

Elias Howe dreamed of being attacked by cannibals. He took note of the cannibals' spears, which had holes near the sharp tips. Howe applied this concept to his new invention, the first working sewing machine. The periodic table of elements was said to have come to the Russian chemist Dmitri Mendeleev during a dream.

Abraham Lincoln, Mark Twain, Mary Shelley, even Adolf Hitler were all influenced by dream events. Whether you're famous or not, dreams are an important part of our lives. Through their power, inspiration, and guidance, dreams are an amazing mystery to us, even today.

Everybody Dreams

You don't need to read this book to discover how exciting dreams are. Just like every human being who has ever lived, you dream. All of us do. It's universal. "Dreaming ties all mankind together," wrote Jack Kerouac. We may differ in many other ways, but one thing we know for sure: No matter our age, race, religion, occupation, diet, or sexual orientation, we all dream, and we do so every single night.

Some people lament that they don't dream. These individuals are sadly mistaken. What they're really saying is that they don't remember their dreams, not that they don't have any. In fact, researchers have found we dream for about two hours each night. Let's take out our trusty calculators, hit some numbers and—holy crap! During a typical lifetime that's an average of six years spent dreaming! Maybe you are one of those individuals who can't remember your dreams at all. Don't worry, you're still having tons of nocturnal adventures, you just have a hard time recalling them upon waking (we'll help with that soon enough).

But why do we dream? Surely there must be some sort of purpose to such a common activity? What are dreams anyway? What is going on when we sleep, and where are we going? In our ultramodern world, with all of our cultural history, understanding, and cleverness, the answer may surprise you.

We don't know.

Understanding Dreams

There have been countless theories that attempt to explain dreams. Modern psychology has been trying to uncover the secret of dreaming since Sigmund Freud lit the proverbial cigar of insight in his turn-of-the-century classic, *The Interpretation of Dreams*. Published in 1899, this work established Freud's stance on dreams and kicked off a massive change in how modern society viewed dreaming.

In a nutshell, Freud claimed that all dreams are forms of wish fulfillment. That is, they stem from our repressed conflicts and desires accumulated throughout life. Dreams are our "unconscious" mind's attempts to resolve these past conflicts.

Since Freud, dozens and dozens of the brightest thinkers have followed in the Austrian's footsteps, attempting to understand this experience we call dreaming. More than a century has passed since *The Interpretation of Dreams* was published, so we must have made a lot of headway, right? Well, sort of. No single consensus has emerged on what dreams are or why we have them. If this seems as crazy to you as it does to us, consider that science is still unraveling the exact purpose and function of sleep itself.

Some researchers suggest that dreams serve no real purpose, while others believe that dreaming is essential to mental, emotional, and physical well-being. Here are some of the main ideas:

🐝 **Our brains are like computers.** Some think dreams are a way for us to organize information and help store memories. Just like a computer, dreams are a way for us to "defragment" and reorganize our minds so that we wake up refreshed and ready to process more information.

🐝 **Future rehearsal.** One theory believes that dreams are simply a safe environment for us to make connections among different thoughts and emotions, a place where we can prepare and practice for upcoming events.

🐝 **Randomness.** If you ever took a psychology course in college, then you've definitely heard about this one. The activation synthesis model, one of the more recognized theories today, was proposed in 1977 by scientists Alan Hobson and Robert McCarley. According to them, dreams are just the brain's reaction to biological processes that occur during sleep. They declared, "Dreams are a by-product of random neural firing . . . our frontal lobe tries to organize it into a storyline." In essence, they are suggesting that dreams are gibberish.

The Dream Experience

Which do you want first, the good news or the bad news? The bad news is that our society is a bit ass-backward when it comes to dreams. Overall, it seems that we don't value them as the amazing gems of human experiences that they are. As Robert Moss puts it in his book *Conscious Dreaming*, "The typical dreamer, after waking, has no more idea where he spent the night than an amnesiac drunk."

Some of us refer to dreams as being "childish," "gibberish," and "a waste of time." That's just the environment we grew up in. We tend to remember only fragments that often make no sense to us. The bad news is that we're told to ignore our dreams, to wave them off as a meaningless distraction.

We would say that the modern dream theories above are not incorrect, but they are incomplete. Science has examined only the ground floor of a twenty-story building; there is much more to learn about the subject. So what's the good news? It doesn't have to be this way. As pioneers, we can change the course we're on and steer the ship in a new direction. We can develop our dreaming skills simply by choosing to do so.

For example, when we say the word *dreams*, what exactly do we mean? Many of us, when groping for a definition, think of fleeting images and vague feelings, random fragments of stories. And why not? We wake up in the morning, or think about a dream later that day, and this is how they seem—wispy and choppy.

But that first impression is only the memory of the dream. The remembered dream is not the dream itself.

This is a very important distinction. If you were to remember, say, your tenth birthday party or what you did two Saturdays ago, what would those memories be like? They would be sort of like a remembered dream: cloudy images, fuzzy or faint feelings, minor details here and there that stick out. The memory of your tenth birthday party would be nothing compared to the actual experience of your tenth birthday. Just like real-life events, dreams themselves are experiences that have a present moment just like now.

Becoming aware of this present moment is the key to lucid dreaming.

Think of a man in a boat, looking at the surface of the ocean. Below he sees blotches of color and shapes moving in the water and concludes that the objects down there are just that, blotches of color and shapes. Then he puts on some scuba gear and goes for a swim.

As he sinks below the surface of the ocean, an entire world surrounds him. The colors and shapes he once thought were only glimmers are vividly alive and detailed. There are fish, coral, and complex ecosystems that have existed all this time, right under his nose.

If we look at dreams from the outside looking in (only the memory of the dream), we will not grasp the full realness of dreams. To understand what dreaming is, we need to dive into the ocean. We need to experience them as they unfold. This is the heart of lucid dreaming—the present-moment awareness of the dream world.

Where Do You Go When You Dream?

No one knows where dreams take place. Sure, scientists and psychologists have theorized and pondered over this daunting question, but an official statement has yet to surface. Take a second and think it over yourself:

Where do I go when I dream? In this book, we tend to call this destination the subconscious. To rashly summarize, the subconscious is the part of our minds that's responsible for anything other than conscious mental activity.

MINCING WORDS

What's the difference between the unconscious and the subconscious? The two words are basically interchangeable; we just happen to prefer *subconscious*. Our hang-up with the more clinical word *unconscious* is that it evokes the image of a comatose, detached vegetable. The word *subconscious*, on the other hand, leads us to imagine a place that is hidden but still well within our reach.

The subconscious is (theoretically) much larger than the conscious mind, and the former feeds into the latter, influencing our decisions, thoughts, and feelings. The subconscious appears to be the source of our imagination, and it may be the well from which wisdom springs. It's an educated guess to say that the dream world is the subconscious incarnate. But since our dreams are a tapestry woven from personal symbols, archetypes, and waking life details, it seems fair to say that the dream world is the actual embodiment of our larger minds.

It's a nice visual, isn't it? Inside your skull is an infinite world filled with clouds, beasts, memories, fears, old friends, and entire cities. And each and every night, you have access to this boundless landscape. Talk about self-exploration! As you become conscious in your dreams, keep this question in mind: Is it the subconscious that we're visiting, or is it somewhere else, somewhere beyond the scope of our current understanding?

This question is not new. For thousands of years, humans have been exploring the mystery of our nocturnal adventures.

3

A History of Dreaming

If we have learned one thing from the history of invention and discovery, it is that, in the long run—and often in the short one— the most daring prophecies seem laughably conservative.

—Arthur C. Clarke,
writer, knight, and scuba diver

S hamanic cultures believed that dreams are a key to realities hidden from our five senses, and that there are many subtle worlds that exist parallel to and overlapping the physical one. To them, dreams were a connection to these higher realities, a bridge to the soul, a journeying to the realm of "spirit." Many aboriginal cultures throughout the world believed in Dreamtime, a separate reality entirely, a collective space where one has direct access to sacred knowledge, and can communicate with the deceased and learn from the spiritual masters who have transcended the physical world.

To many indigenous cultures, such as the Iroquois, someone who was not in touch with their dreams was not in touch with their soul. Not only were dreams important, but they were also vital. If you were disconnected from your dreams you were considered a spiritual and emotional cripple. Ouch!

If these ideas fly in the face of everything you were ever taught about dreaming, we're right there with you. It's hard to understand what these ancients were talking about. Other worlds? Meeting other people in dreams? What are you on, drugs? The ideas sound crazy to us now.

To understand where these ancients were coming from, we need to first humor the idea that dreams are important, whatever they are. With minds open, let's take a short peek at how past cultures saw dreaming. Despite the many perspectives you'll see, the majority of cultures would agree on one thing: Dreams are anything but meaningless.

Sumerians

The earliest evidence of dreaming dates all the way back to 3100 BCE in the Fertile Crescent of Mesopotamia. Through the recorded stories of legendary Gilgamesh, we read of the king's recurring dreams of his goddess-mother, Ninsun, dreams that were taken as prophecy and used to guide the king's decisions in the waking world. It's clear from these stories that dreams have been playing a historical role for at least the past five thousand years.

Ancient Egyptians

The first recorded evidence of a dreaming society can be found among the ancient Egyptians. These guys believed dreams to be a direct connection to the spirit world. The Egyptians appear to have practiced a form of lucid dreaming and likely mastered dream skills such as shape-shifting and time travel. How do we know they were conscious dreamers? One clear indicator comes from their belief in the Ba (or soul), which they thought could travel consciously outside of the body while the body slept. Even their word for dreams, *rswt* (pronounced "resut"), translates as "awakening" or "to come awake" and was depicted in hieroglyphs as an open eye. Scholars say that the open eye might also signify an awakening to truths, advice, or insights commonly missed in daily waking life.

Egyptians were so into dreams that they constructed temples specifically for the practice of dream incubation, a method of receiving divine healing and revelatory messages through sleep. They believed that the dream world was a deeper reality, a place where true transformation could happen. The dream interpreters of their day were called the "Masters of the Secret Things." Imagine that on a business card.

Ancient Greeks

Ancient Greeks saw dreams as a spiritual practice as well, a connection to the divine. At first, only Zeus was thought to send divine dreams, but as time went on, other gods were allowed to send dreams too. There were two gods who specifically ruled in the arena of dreaming— Hypnos presided over sleep, and his son, Morpheus, ruled dreams. Scattered across the Mediterranean, the Greeks built more than three hundred shrines to serve as dream temples. These temples were heavily involved with dream healing, where the sick came to heal physically, emotionally, and spiritually with the help of nightly dreams.

Well over two thousand years before Freud, Plato theorized that dreams are the expression of our repressed desires. In his volume *The Republic,* Plato wrote that "in all of us, even the most highly respectable, there is a lawless wild beast nature, which peers out in sleep." Aristotle, on the other hand, while fascinated by the fact that we can perceive colors, lights, and images with our eyes closed during sleep, concluded that dreams had no purpose. They foretell the future, you say? Mere coincidence.

In the second century BCE, Artemidorus wrote his five-volume work, *Oneirocritica.* "The crocodile signifies a pirate, murderer or a man who is no less wicked," he wrote. "The way in which the crocodile treats the dreamer determines the way in which he will be treated by the person who is represented by the crocodile. The cat signifies an adulterer. For it is a bird-thief. And birds resemble women." Instead of creating just a generic interpretation system of dreams, Artemidorus was the first to take the individual's personal background into account.

Romans

Like many aspects of their culture, the Romans piggybacked their dream beliefs off the ancient Greeks and Egyptians. They had everything from dream incubation to dream temples, they even read the *Oneirocritica.* Pythagoreanism, a Greek philosophy dating back as far as 500 BCE, was also revived by the Romans.

This metaphysical system of belief was based on mathematics but had nothing to do with high school–level geometry. It stated that "conscious soul travel" was possible and that spiritual gurus born centuries apart could communicate through these mystical avenues. As more and more Romans were converted to Christianity, dream interpretation was refocused through the lens of the Bible, and the dream temple culture was all but wiped out.

Hindus

According to Hindu mythology, everything around us in the physical world is a dream happening in Vishnu's mind. Even we ourselves are only manifestations, dream characters if you will. It is thought that our world will end when Vishnu's dream ends. "Dreaming gives us a glimpse of the god who creates us by dreaming us into existence." Hindus believe that dreaming is a higher state of consciousness than the waking state.

Tibetans

The philosophical practice of dream yoga among the Tibetan Buddhists dates back at least a thousand years. While ancient Egyptians and Greeks knew the power of dreams, these yogis were the pioneers of lucid dreaming—we can't thank them enough for laying the groundwork. They described specific techniques for achieving lucidity and training consciousness. The buck didn't stop at lucid dreaming either. Once they became aware in the dream state, yogis had to complete a number of tasks, progressing to higher levels of their practice. These challenges included the exploration of various "worlds," speaking with enlightened dream beings, and shape-shifting into other animals, to name just a few. The ultimate goal for a dream yogi was to become conscious of the fact that "all life is but a dream." "Apprehending the dream" was a term that meant attaining complete conscious awareness. If a practitioner could become really, really aware in a dream, they thought, the dream would bleed together into a big mix of egoless bliss. *Ah, pure nothingness.* Once a yogi entered this nothingness, he would be able to observe the absolute purest form of conscious awareness.

Chinese

Recorded evidence of dreaming in Chinese culture dates back to over four thousand years ago. Like other cultures from that era, the Chinese idea of dreams intertwined with other concepts: the realm of the dead and of the spirit. They divided the soul into two parts, the *p'o* (material soul) and the *hun* (spiritual soul). At night, when the physical body was at rest, the spiritual soul would depart from the body. The *hun* was free to visit the land of the dead or commune with the souls of other dreamers. (Just don't wake someone up before their soul comes back to their body. The Chinese believed that their soul could be lost if they were awakened too abruptly, and no one wants that.)

Hebrews

The deeper you go into the history of the Hebraic culture, the more you'll find clues to a dreaming culture. In the Talmud, a book written between 200 and 500 CE that instructs one on how to apply the Torah to everyday life, there are over two hundred references to dreams. It even has a dream dictionary of sorts that allows the reader to analyze dreams, nightmares, and visions. It states that "dreams which are not understood are like letters which are not opened." Dreaming was considered to be a direct way to receive guidance from God.

Indigenous Tribes

To these "people of the earth," everything around us contained spirit and we accessed this spirit realm when we dreamed. Dreaming was also a very social activity. These cultures thought that when we dream, we go to a shared realm that is not limited by space or time. One could have dream visitors in addition to visiting other people's dreams. Instead of gulping down a cup of joe, both Aboriginal Australians and the Iroquois would start their day by sharing their adventures of the previous night. Dreams were often a source of guidance not only for the individual, but also for an entire community, and were used in hunting, healing, and war.

European Middle Ages

They aren't called the Dark Ages for nothing. As the dogmatic practices of Christianity spread throughout Europe, dreams began taking a backseat. Despite this unfortunate approach to dreams during this time, it's important to note that in the religious texts of Christianity there are plenty of nods to dreaming. Dig and you will find stories of divine dreams and the interpretations that followed. There are hundreds of dreams in the Bible alone. As Christianity continued to spread during this time, dreams were looked on as being evil and sinful. Martin Luther spread the word that the devil was responsible for dreams and that divine messages could only be received through the church. St. John Chrysostom stated that dreams were insubstantial. Come on, guys, really?

Modern Times

After the Dark Ages dreaming was basically swept under the rug. Anthropologist Raymond L. M. Lee notes that even after the Renaissance "dreams were treated as unremarkable by-products of psychological disturbances or bad digestion that possessed no real value." It wasn't until the turn of the twentieth century that dreams were brought out of the darkness by our friend Dr. Sigmund Freud. He started an entire branch of psychology devoted to unlocking his patients' "unconscious" minds through the interpretation of dreams.

Not only had the dust been brushed off the topic, but dreams were now also seen in an entirely new light—they were secular.

Some of Freud's ideas were soon challenged by his own student, a radically thinking upstart named Carl Jung. Dr. Jung believed that dreams were not only about the past, but about the present too. He felt that dreams show us what we are striving to achieve as well as what stands in our way.

Jung didn't completely abandon his teacher's thoughts. He accepted Freud's basic structure and his theories on the language of dreaming, along with the idea of interpreting dreams through associations. And Jung wasn't just observing patients; he was an ardent dreamer. Take a look at his academic essays and you'll find some surprising topics: psychic powers, collective dreaming, and telepathy. He believed we dreamed in the collective unconscious (a shared space), and he coined the terms *archetype* and *synchronicity*. Thanks to Jung, a lot of modern-day dream explorers were inspired to think out of the box, exhuming ideas that had been buried since the ancients.

PENNY FOR YOUR THOUGHTS

What do you think? Are dreams private, separate experiences happening only in each of our minds? Or is it possible that dreams take place in a shared and collective place? As we have seen, many cultures believed the latter to be true.

Who Has It Right?

Our ancestors had a totally different relationship to dreaming than we do today. Dreams were an extension of the waking world, a reality just as important as "real life." Most of us have been conditioned since childhood to look at these inner world visions as "just dreams." You don't have to believe any of the ideas that you just read, but we suggest considering them as possibilities, no matter how alien they may seem.

Before writing this book, before we did some investigation into the matter, we thought we knew what dreams were. Now, some of the ancients' ideas don't sound so crazy to us.

So let's do ourselves a favor and start from scratch. Imagine a giant chalkboard filled with everything you know or think about dreams, covered with words and diagrams, crammed and overlapping with ideas. Now take a sponge, dip it in water, and run it across the blackboard. Erase everything. Good. To relearn how to dream all you'll need is an open mind.

As our mothers taught us, believe nothing that you hear and only half of what you see. Do not take our word, the words of our ancestors, or even the words of modern psychology as gospel. Instead, discover for yourself through experience what dreams really are.

The following chapters will give you the practical guidance you need to become lucid. We'll start with some basics, reconnecting you with your nighttime journeys. No more wispy, cloudy dreams for you. As you progress, you'll begin to notice that your dreams take on a potent and vivid quality; the memories will be more complete.

PART TWO

PACKING YOUR BAGS

hen we first took the journey to the dream world and learned how to become lucid, the process wasn't very simple. We found numerous books and websites on the subject, each offering a laundry list of techniques. We felt that these sources of information didn't speak to us; many were too academic in tone and focus. The ones that weren't dense and complicated seemed to lack a straightforward path—they would offer many different options and let you experiment and see what worked. We found ourselves lost in the jungle, trying this way and that. In the end, we did learn to lucid dream, and discovered brilliant techniques along the way. But looking back, we saw that the road doesn't need to be all that complicated.

As your guides, we don't want you to go through the same laborious process. We've decided to boil down all the numerous techniques out there and present to you only the best. As we venture forth, it's important that we give you a well-equipped toolbox filled with the basics of lucid dreaming. We won't tell you more (or less) than what you need to know.

In this section you will learn how to reconnect to your dreams, if you have lost touch with them, as so many of us have. You will learn the single most powerful technique for inducing lucidity. By the end of this section, you'll be ready to jump into your own subconscious and start exploring it. Take your time. To master lucid dreaming, you first need to remember your dreams, learn the art of a good intention, and build a healthy suspicion of reality.

It's just like learning to sail a boat. Before you become an expert skipper, you need to learn how to steer the boat, how to catch the wind, and what to do when you capsize. Master the boat and you shall master the sea. Ahoy dreams!

4

The REM Stage

~ • ~

*For the function of the brain which, during sleep, conjures up a completely
objective, perceptible, and even palpable world must have just as large
a share in the presentation of the objective world of our waking hours.
For both worlds, although different in their matter,
are nonetheless made from the same mould.*

—Arthur Schopenhauer,
pessimistic German philosopher

You're trying to catch a train to a faraway place. You run through the doors of the station and lift your arm to check your watch, but when the steam whistle blows you know that there's only a minute to spare. Heart pounding, if your feet aren't quick enough to reach the platform in time, the train will chug away without you. The window of time is closing quickly.

You see the train now, smoke pouring from its top. All aboard! Out of breath, you leap through the air.

"Next stop, dreams!"

Safely on board, you take your seat. The rhythmic clickety-clack of the wheels relaxes your body, and though you're not quite sure where you're heading, you're excited to be going there all the same.

We've explored the idea of what dreams are, but when do they happen? Let's scribble three letters onto our clean and empty blackboard: *R-E-M*. No, we're not talking about the 1990s pop-rock sensation, we're talking about the stage of sleep where dreams occur. These modest letters couldn't be more important for a lucid dreamer. Let's find out why.

Back in the early 1950s, Eugene Aserinsky was dead broke and trying to support his family. Even though he never obtained an undergraduate degree, he had managed to convince the University of Chicago to let him attend as a graduate student. Dusting off an old EEG machine found in the basement of a university building, Aserinsky hooked electrodes to the scalp of his son, Armond, studying his sleeping patterns. The young wannabe scientist took note of some curious readouts. During certain periods of the night, Armond's sleeping brain would suddenly shift, as if his brain were wide awake.

Aserinsky had a good idea what was causing this anomaly: His machine was broken. "If I had a suicidal nature, this would have been the time," Aserinsky recalled. "I was married, I had a child, I'd been in universities for twelve years with no degree to show for it. I'd already spent a couple of years horsing around on this. I was absolutely finished."

But after several more studies with additional subjects, the anomaly seemed to be real enough. He brought in a veteran sleep scientist, Nathaniel Kleitman, and the two began to notice that during this stage of sleep the heart rate and breathing quickened and blood pressure rose. They noted that about four or five times during a given night, their subjects' brains would suddenly shift, like a radio changing its frequency, to a very active and "wakeful" brain state. At the same time, the subject's eyes would move rapidly back and forth under closed lids.

The results of these experiments led to one of the biggest breakthroughs in the scientific study of dreams. The two men proved that despite previous thinking, dreaming is not synonymous with sleep—dreaming occurs during a specific time *within* sleep.

When it was time to name their discovery, they did what any self-respecting scientist would do and gave it an incredibly boring name: Rapid Eye Movement sleep (REM for short). However, even with a dull name, the discovery was profound. The bridge between the waking world and the dream world was found in the eye of the beholder. Science had figured out *when* we dream.

ONE BRAIN, TWO WORLDS

The dreaming brain might be more similar to our waking brain than we think. Professors Llinás and Paré at New York University argue that REM sleep and wakefulness are essentially similar brain states. The only difference is in the sensory stimuli coming in. During the day our experience is shaped by the sensory input coming from the external world, but when we dream our attention is turned inward. Our thoughts and memories become the active agents in creating our experience.

REM and Stages of Sleep

While we don't know for sure why we dream, we do know some science about the nature of sleep. Throughout the night, we cycle through two main phases of sleep: non-REM and REM. Non-REM (also known as slow wave sleep) is characterized by slow brain waves. Imagine it like a roller coaster—we rise and fall between different stages of sleep like the up-and-down journey of a thrill ride.

In the beginning hours of sleep, our REM (dream time) is relatively short, five to ten minutes at the most. Most of our sleep occurs in non-REM. However, as the night progresses, the amount of time spent in REM increases. By morning, the other stages of sleep disappear, and depending on how much sleep you get, your last two REM stages can last up to fifty minutes each! Here's how a typical night goes:

Stage 1: As you lie in bed and begin to feel your body dozing off, you are already entering the first stage of sleep. This stage is the bridge between our waking and dreaming selves. During this transition, you may experience images, lights, or other sensations, which are known as hypnagogic imagery. This is the time where you may experience hypnic jerks, those random twitches you get where you kick or spasm just before drifting off, a natural occurrence that your dog or spouse may know all too well. This stage is commonly known as twilight (think more Rod Serling than vampires).

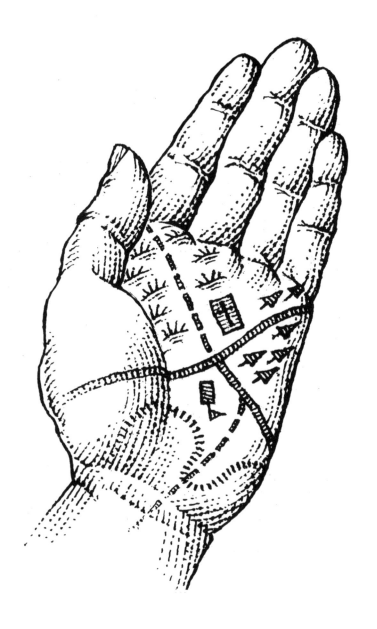

Stage 2: This is your body's prep stage. Here you've already fallen asleep, but you aren't quite in a deep sleep yet. Toward the end of this stage, as you prepare for deep sleep, your body begins to lower your heart rate as well as your core temperature. Things are beginning to slooooowwww dooooowwwwn. No dreams here, my friend.

Stage 3: Welcome to repair mode. At this point you're in deep sleep. Like a computer rebooting itself, your body is rebuilding muscle and bone mass, making repairs to organs and tissue, and strengthening your immune system.

We then begin our ascent back toward waking and away from deep sleep. Like a roller coaster, we climb back up to the level of stage two . . . then one . . . then . . .

REM Stage: Finally! The fun stuff! Your brain is buzzing with activity, and it seems like you're about to wake up, but the roller coaster plateaus and you enter the sweet spot—the dream zone. In fact, your brain activity is so similar to being awake that if a scientist was only monitoring your noggin, he or she would have a hard time knowing whether you're awake or dreaming. You just entered the most important stage for the lucid dreamer—the very seat of dreams.

All Aboard!

It would be hard to catch a train if you didn't know when it was leaving. But if you know the departure time, it's easy enough to jump on board before it pushes off into the distance. Similarly, it's important to know when REM sleep happens because that's when you're dreaming the most. To a lucid dreamer, this information is pure gold. If you know when you dream, you can home all your lucid dreaming energy at that one target, increasing your odds of hitting a bull's-eye. Deliberately catching your last cycle of REM sleep is one of the best tools for inducing a lucid dream, one that we'll come back to in the coming chapters. The last fifty-minute cycle, those dreams in the early morning hours, is where our journey begins.

Summary

Dreaming occurs mainly in what is known as REM sleep.

- When we enter REM, our brain shows patterns similar to wakefulness.

- With no external stimuli shaping our reality, we turn inward, creating our experience from our thoughts and memories.

- Knowing when REM occurs will be one of the most powerful tools for inducing lucid dreams.

5

The Power of Intention

Who looks outside, dreams;
who looks inside, awakes.

—Carl Jung,
founder of analytical psychology,
truly a modern-day shaman

Some people are natural lucid dreamers. For them, being aware during the dream state is something they did as a kid and continue to do throughout their lives. For others, it must be learned.

When we started teaching people how to lucid dream, we were surprised by a recurring event: People would often have their first lucid dream just after discovering that lucid dreaming existed. It was as if once they knew to look for it, it was much easier to find.

It makes sense, doesn't it? In the early 1950s, the world record for the mile race was over four minutes. It had been floating just above the 4-minute mark for over ten years, and the public didn't think a man could physically run a mile faster than that.

But on a windy May day in 1954, Englishman Roger Bannister broke the record at 3 minutes 59.4 seconds. Only six weeks later, an Aussie named John Landy broke Bannister's record with 3:58. Then, later that same summer, Bannister and Landy went head-to-head in a dramatic race-off. Bannister narrowly won and reclaimed his record. Today, we're still pushing the boundaries of what's possible with a world record held by Hicham El Guerrouj at a whopping 3:43!

It's tough to bushwhack through a dense forest. But once the path is cut, others can follow much more easily. Before you can achieve a goal, you have to know what that goal is and that it's possible to achieve. You have to set an intention.

The same holds true for lucid dreaming. Once you set an intention to go to sleep and to wake up within your dreams, it becomes much easier to do. It's all about cultivating this strong desire.

This guide will teach you the tools you need to achieve lucidity, but nothing is more useful than having the burning desire to become lucid. Whether you want to remember your dreams, incubate a specific dream, induce lucidity, or master any other technique, intention is key. It is the foundation of lucid dreaming.

So What Is an Intention?

An intention is a purpose, a goal. A directed thought toward a specific action. We set intentions all the time in waking life: to eat healthier, become physically fit, work less, play more, learn a new language. When we lack intentions in life (or in dreams), we sometimes wander meaninglessly and without direction. We become vague and unspecific about what we want. How many of us struggle with this problem when it comes to our careers or our personal lives? When we're clear about what it is we want, it's a whole lot easier to go out and get it.

Don't worry, we won't ask you to jot down all your life goals. Fortunately, you already know what you want: to become lucid in a dream. With this clear desire in mind, let's look at the most effective ways to set an intention.

The Power of Thought

Have you ever heard of athletes mentally rehearsing as an important part of their practice? Well, it's possible that this isn't just superstition; science is finding out some pretty interesting stuff, proving just how influential the mind can be over its surroundings.

A study was done in which skiers were hooked up to an electromyograph (EMG), an instrument that measures the activity of electrical waves associated with the skeletal muscles. The skiers were asked to carry out mental rehearsals of themselves skiing. The skiers were then told to visualize themselves performing their runs on the slopes in their mind's eye. What the researchers found was that the electrical impulses of the athlete's muscles were the same as the ones they used when they were actually skiing.

"The brain sent the same instructions to the body whether the skiers were simply thinking of a particular movement or actually carrying it out," writes Lynn McTaggart in *The Intention*

Experiment. "Thought produced the same mental instructions as action." In other words, their brain did not differentiate between a thought and a real-life event.

Guang Yue, an exercise psychologist at the Cleveland Clinic Foundation, was also interested in the power of thought. All you couch potatoes out there, listen up: He found that simply imagining exercise can significantly increase muscle strength. You read right! He had a control group go to the gym and work their biceps while another group simply imagined doing so. By just thinking about it, the average subject who imagined the workout had increased muscle strength by 13.5 percent while the subjects who went to the gym increased muscle strength by 30 percent. Throw away that gym membership that you never use anyway and stick with some focused thought.

We don't need scientific experiments to tell us how powerful thoughts are. Our lives are run by the intentions swirling around in our heads. Even a small goal, such as baking a cake, begins with a specific intention in mind. You first imagine what ingredients you'll use, the different steps along the way, and how delicious the cake will be when it's done.

Larger goals, such as starting a business, need more passion and specificity, but the process still begins with an intention, a burning desire to get what you want.

For us lucid dreamers, not only do clear, passionate, and specific thoughts prove essential as we explore our dreams, but they are often necessary to becoming lucid in the first place.

How to Set an Intention

You can have anything you want if you want it desperately enough. You must want it with an inner exuberance that erupts through the skin and joins the energy that created the world.

—Sheila Graham,
gossip columnist during Hollywood's "Golden Age,"
never got over F. Scott Fitzgerald

A strong intention is filled with passion, what dream author Robert Moss calls "juice." It should be soaked in electricity, powered by excitement. An intention is a bird in your stomach, fanning your flame with each flap of its wings. Stop for a moment and realize the profound nature of lucid dreaming. Imagine how incredible it would be to wake up in a dream, head into your own inner universe, to walk around and explore.

With complete self-reflection and conscious freedom, you can do anything you want. Excited yet? Follow these steps to set an effective intention—but remember that an intention isn't a mathematical equation, it's a heartfelt desire.

1. **Wording is key.** To be most effective, an intention should be highly specific. Create short, powerful statements that focus your desire. These are commonly known as affirmations. Your affirmation should be clear and direct. If you say, for example, "I would like to someday learn the piano," well then, someday you might. A specific version of that idea is, "On Tuesday I will start piano lessons and learn scales before June." Try phrasing your intention in the present tense as if it has already occurred. For example, before bed say to yourself, "I am lucid and aware in my dream." Thinking in the present tense eliminates any doubt that your wish will come true.

2. **Feel it, see it.** All you Harry Potter nerds out there know this spellbinding lesson: Words are meaningless unless you actually feel them. "I will become lucid in my dreams tonight." When you state your intention, picture your desire coming to fruition—actually imagine yourself in a dream realizing that it's a dream. It might be helpful to think of a recurring dream that you have and pretend that you're back in that very situation. Visualize the inner world that surrounds you. Feel what that sensation is like, that exciting "aha" moment: I'm lucid!

Engage all five senses—imagine breathing dream air, flying, looking around. The more clearly you can imagine, the better.

When you were a kid, you played "make-believe." You probably imagined yourself battling dragons. By seeing the dragon in front of you, by feeling the excitement of the battle, by allowing yourself to be lost in that moment, it was real.

3. **Expectation.** An advanced lucid dreamer doesn't just go to sleep hoping that a spontaneous lucid dream will happen. Instead he goes to bed looking for a lucid dream. In other words, he expects to wake up in his dream that night. You sleep every night, and dream for about two hours. Multiply that digit by days and weeks and suddenly you've got a lot of practice time on your hands.

4. **Make it your dominant thought.** Throughout this guide, we'll often ask you to use an intention before bed. It's important that these thoughts, feelings, and affirmations be the last things on your mind as you go to sleep. If you find yourself thinking about something else, simply let those thoughts go and gently bring your mind back to your focused intention. "I am lucid and aware in my dream." Concentrate on your intention until sleep pulls you under. This way your desire will carry over into the dream world and produce the exact result you are hoping for.

GRATITUDE

How can we expect something will happen if it hasn't happened already? One word: *gratitude*. Feeling thankful before something happens is a very powerful, creative force. And it's not some mystical mumbo-jumbo nonsense. If you're thankful for something in advance, it has already happened in your mind, eliminating any stress and fears that come with the unknown. As you visualize yourself in the dream in the present moment, imagine yourself looking around at the dream world in front of you. Give thanks for the lucid dream prior to actually experiencing it. Even say out loud, "thank you," and let those goose bumps run down your spine. Ahhhh, feels good.

I Caught a Big One!

An effective intention is all about bringing a future goal closer to the present moment, like a fisherman reeling in a fish, dragging it through the water toward his boat. The better the intention, the less space there is between you and your goal, the more real and tangible it is. All that is required to become lucid is to go to bed with the confidence, expectation, and intention to realize when you are dreaming.

You are dreaming every night, unconscious and unaware that you're inside a dream. Begin now to look for awareness in your dreams. If you do, you might be surprised to actually find it.

This is one of the greatest paradoxes: The very thing for which you are looking is actually essential to finding it. Chew on that one for a while.

Summary

- Many people have their first lucid dream directly after hearing or reading about it.

- The mind doesn't know the difference between a thought and an action. Therefore it's important to mentally rehearse becoming lucid.

- Visualize yourself in a dream, feeling the excitement of recognizing the dream state.

- Feel a sense of gratitude that you have experienced a lucid dream before having one.

- When setting an intention, make a simple phrase to go along with it, such as "I am aware and lucid in my dream."

- Cultivate a strong desire to lucid dream and make such desires your dominant thoughts before bed.

6

Remembering
Your Dreams

~•~

Let us learn to dream, gentlemen, and then we may perhaps find the truth.

—F. A. Keule, German chemist,
discovered more in dreams than most do awake

A loud alarm clock jolts you awake. You struggle to reach for the off button. Snooze? Wait, is it a phone call? Who's calling this early? You stumble out of bed and into the bathroom, dreams lingering, barely holding on by a thread. What was I just dreaming about? The memory fades quickly as you begin to think about your day, your responsibilities, your obligations. You try to pull a piece, an image, anything from your memory but to no avail.

Sadly, so many of our nighttime adventures disappear like this, sinking into the waters like wrecked ships, never to be salvaged. If you never remember your dreams or rarely do, don't fret.

There's nothing wrong with you or your ability to dream. You are a healthy, wonderful, normal human and have many dreams each night, we assure you of that. Your sails are intact; you just need to find the rope to pull and catch the wind.

In other words, you simply need to remember the dreams you're already having.

It might seem obvious, but remembering your dreams goes hand in hand with lucid dreaming. How do you expect to become conscious in your dreams if you can't even remember them? Imagine a wide river, with dreams on one side and your daily life on the other. By remembering your dreams, you build a bridge to the dream world, carrying back memories and experiences across the great divide. Without this connection, you're left on that muddy riverbank alone. You need to have a solid relationship with your dreams before you can become lucid. Building this bridge, strengthening your dream recall, is the first step.

It makes our eyes water just thinking about all those dreams we had that were never remembered, as if a case of amnesia swept away years of our lives. Think of all that wisdom and guidance lost because of bad dream recall (cue the violins).

Despite their fluid and fleeting nature, there are a few simple strategies, an appropriate mind-set that makes remembering your dreams a breeze.

You Are a Dreamer

Anyone . . . who pays attention to his dreams over a period of time will have more dreams than usual—which no doubt means that he remembers his dreams with greater ease and frequency.

—Sigmund Freud,
psychologist, dream pioneer, lover of Greek literature

F or many, remembering dreams seems impossible. We've heard it countless times before: "I don't dream," "I'm a light sleeper," or "I just don't dream as much as other people." Statements like these are double-edged swords. Remember how powerful our words and beliefs can be? By telling yourself that you don't dream or that you never remember, you are in effect creating the exact circumstances to make this belief true. Regardless of your beliefs, however, you must accept this simple fact of life: You and everyone else on this planet dream every single night. The only question now is whether you're doing so consciously or unconsciously.

Dreams Are Real Experiences

W e often think of dreams as these fragmented and foggy images that we only sometimes recall after waking up. As we said earlier, this is not the dream, but only the memory of the dream. It might sound crazy, but dreams are real experiences similar to the events and actions in our waking world. As we travel through our dreams, the experiences are vivid and pristine, so much so that it doesn't occur to us that we might be dreaming. It isn't until we wake up that the memories of the dream, the bits we recall afterward, become cloudy.

Science backs us up on this point. A 2011 Italian study watched the brain activity of participants when they remembered dreams. It notes "the neurophysiological mechanisms underlying the encoding and recall of episodic memories may remain the same across different states of consciousness." In layman's terms, this means that our brains look pretty much the same whether we're remembering waking-life events or whether we're remembering dreams.

SHOW AND TELL

The Achuar Indians, of the Ecuadoran Amazon, share their dreams every morning. They believe their dreams do not belong to the individual but to the entire community. If someone has a bad dream about someone in the tribe, for example, both parties are responsible for coming together and resolving any sort of conflict the dream might be hinting at. Sharing and talking about your dreams with family and friends is a great way to improve dream recall. Practice like the Achuar and create a safe environment where you can talk about your dreams with other people, receive helpful feedback, and always remember to be supportive of others sharing their dreams. You will see your dream recall increase significantly.

Going to Sleep

Remembering your dreams isn't rocket science. You simply need to make the effort. After you have accepted the understanding that you are in fact dreaming every night, it's important to go to sleep trying to remember your nocturnal experiences. Set an intention to remember your dreams before bed. It does wonders.

Set an Intention

1. **Repeat your affirmation.** As you fall asleep, focus your intent on a simple and concise phrase. It should be brief and straightforward: "I remember my dreams." Repeat this affirmation as you drift off to sleep. If you find your mind wandering to other topics, gently nudge it back.

2. **Visualize.** Picture yourself waking up in the morning and recalling your dreams in vivid detail, writing down the details of your dream in your dream journal (see Chapter 7). Before drifting off, see the dream journal page flooded with multiple dreams, vivid experiences, and details.

3. Feel it. Feel yourself coming out of a vivid dream, your eyes opening and your heart still pounding, your head filled with sensations.

Once you get into the habit of remembering your dreams, you won't need to do this exercise each night. You will naturally and automatically begin to remember more and more.

Healthy Sleeping Habits

No doubt about it, lucid dreamers are good sleepers. The following techniques aren't only good for your ability to dream, they're good for your health.

1. Set up nighttime rituals. Do something that will relax you, such as take a hot shower or read. Meditate, draw, stretch, light incense, make a to-do list for tomorrow. Do you follow suit with 50 percent of Americans and watch TV before falling asleep? A recent study wags the finger at you, concluding that watching the tube before bed is one of the two main factors in sleep loss.

2. Go to bed at the same time every night. By going to bed at the same time every night, you'll have more consistent sleep cycles, which will come in handy later for inducing lucid dreams.

3. Bed, bath, and the great beyond. Your bedding is important. Your bedroom should be dark, comfortable, and quiet. It should feel safe, your own private sanctuary where you can go to feel calm and peaceful.

4. Make Grandma proud. Alcohol, tobacco, marijuana, and coffee actually affect your dreaming negatively. Each substance has a different side effect, such as suppressing REM and extending the stage of deep sleep. You certainly don't have to change your lifestyle completely, but since these substances are not conducive to dreaming, try to minimize your intake while preparing for a lucid dream.

Waking Up

I've dreamt in my life dreams that have stayed with me ever after,
and changed my ideas; they've gone through and through me, like wine
through water, and altered the colour of my mind.

—Emily Brontë, English writer, aka Ellis Bell

As we said earlier, in the dream state things are very real when they're happening. It isn't until we wake up that they become fragmented or clouded. Therefore, waking up is one of the most important components in excellent dream recall. Nothing, and we mean nothing, fades the memory of a dream faster than waking up too quickly.

Follow these guidelines to properly wake up and you'll be on the road to remembering long and vivid details. Here's how to do it:

1. Wake slowly and motionlessly. Upon awakening, don't move. Don't even open your eyes. Lie completely still and remain relaxed.

Avoid any abrupt movements. As you emerge from sleep, allow yourself time to remember the dream you were just in. Don't get caught up in your daily responsibilities just yet, there will be a whole day for that. Throw your net in the water, pull it out, and see what you've caught. Let your mind drift back to your dreams and recall everything you can, even if the memories are tiny fragments.

2. Collect fragments. If you can't remember the dream in its entirety (few can), start with what you do remember. Our memory often works by association, so if you can remember one thing, it's very likely you'll remember more. Soon the memory will expand by itself like a snowball, gaining momentum and power. Ask yourself, "What can I remember?" and work your way backward or forward from there.

3. Switch sleeping positions. If you're still hitting a memory blockade, try switching sleeping positions. Lie on your side, roll onto your back, go to your stomach, but do so slowly. You can often recall the experience more easily by lying in the position in which you had the dream.

4. Look to your emotions. If you can't remember a scenario or piece together a plot, it's useful to take note of your emotions. What feelings are currently running through you? Was your dream good or bad? Your emotions are a great indicator of the kind of dream you were just having. If you can't remember anything, write down how you're feeling and any thoughts going through your mind. This practice may trigger more memories as well.

5. Write them down. Finally, write down your dreams. This aspect of dreaming is so important that the entire next chapter is dedicated to it. There is no way around this fact: If you want to become lucid in your dreams, you need to record your nighttime adventures.

A 2003 study by professor David Watson observed 193 college students over a few months, asking each day if they remembered any dreams. Here is Watson's conclusion: "Dream recall was specifically associated with openness. . . . Analyses indicated that individuals who are prone to absorption, imagination and fantasy are particularly likely to remember their dreams and to report other vivid nocturnal experiences." In other words, if we would just open up to our dreams, they will come flooding in.

Summary

- The dream you remember in the morning is just the memory of the dream, not the dream itself.

- Dreams are real experiences we are having every night. Because of poor dream recall, we're forgetting about a whole other life that we are part of.

- Remembering your dreams takes a shift in priority and focus. Value your dreams as important experiences that you want to begin remembering and they will blossom.

- Begin practicing good sleeping habits, such as consistent bedtimes and getting plenty of rest.

- Set an intention before bed: "I will remember my dreams."

- Practice waking up correctly: slow and motionlessly.

- Before you attempt to have a lucid dream, it's important that you remember at least one dream a night.

7

Keeping a
Dream Journal

*While I viewed these mountains I felt a secret pleasure in finding myself
so near the head of the heretofore conceived boundless Missouri; but when
I reflected on the difficulties which this snowy barrier would most probably
throw in my way to the Pacific, and the sufferings and hardships of myself
and party in them, it in some measure counterbalanced the joy I had felt
in the first moments in which I gazed on them; but as I have always held
it a crime to anticipate evils I will believe it a good comfortable road
until I am compelled to believe differently.*

—Meriwether Lewis (of Lewis and Clark),
explorer, soldier, and bear fighter

Great explorers always keep a log of their adventures.
Lewis and Clark kept a journal as they ventured into the
American frontier. Charles Darwin retold the tale of his
time on the HMS *Beagle*. Even Captain Kirk had his star-dated
captain's log. A pioneer's mission was to catalog the details of a

foreign land. They noted the features of the landscapes, the attitudes of the locals, and the twists and turns of various adventures. As explorers, we will do the same. Keeping a dream journal is not about writing down the foggy memories of a nighttime slumber, but about recounting the story of one's experiences from a completely other world.

Just like Lewis and Clark, just like Darwin and Captain Kirk, we will be venturing into a new world. Unfortunately, we can't bring back any samples, T-shirts, or shot glasses. The only souvenirs that can be retrieved are our memories, what can be written with pen and paper.

Improve Dream Recall

Experts say that people typically forget more than 50 percent of their dreams within five minutes of waking up. Within ten minutes, 90 percent is lost. This is why it's important not only to write down your dreams but also to do so as soon as you wake up.

Funny enough, writing down your dreams is also the single most effective way to recall them. By recording them, you're essentially saying, "Hey subconscious! Dreams are important. I'm writing them down because I want to remember them!" It may sound counterintuitive, but this is an extremely common occurrence—just by keeping a dream journal, you will naturally begin to remember longer, more vivid dreams. And all you have to do is pick up a pen.

A DREAMING SAINT

Le Marquis Saint-Denys was a French sinologist in the nineteenth century and one of the most recognized oneironauts. He started recording his dreams at age thirteen, eventually accumulating more than 1,946 in total. Saint-Denys believed that anyone could achieve lucidity in their dreams and developed techniques for inducing them. After six months of practicing his own exercises, he was achieving lucidity two nights a week. Keeping a dream journal and familiarizing yourself with your dreams, he believed, was one of his most useful techniques.

How to Keep a Dream Journal

If you don't already have one, you'll want to get a nice-looking journal that you can write your dreams in. It will contain the workings of your inner world, so show it a little respect. Don't use some small pad of paper; you'll make a mess of it.

If you're like us, you've kept a dream journal on and off throughout your life, but you're busy, and when the alarm clock rings in the morning, writing down your dreams could mean that you'd be late for work or school. What's the point of scribbling down these events? Recording your dreams can seem frivolous and impractical, but this feeling couldn't be further from the truth.

Personally, as we became lucid dreamers, we had to embrace our dream journals with open arms. Our journals allowed us to remember more dreams, reveal what's going on in our inner worlds, and most important, trigger lucid dreams. The value of keeping a dream journal far exceeds the effort put into keeping one. If dreams are messages from our subconscious, then they have important information to deliver. Ignore these messages and watch dreams disappear from your life completely. Like a needy lover, they want your attention, and if you cut them off, they'll respond with the silent treatment.

The following tips may seem like common sense, but they're important nonetheless.

🐝 Keep It Next to Your Bed

Keep your journal and a pen close to your bed in the same consistent spot, so that when the morning comes, you don't have to go on a memory-fading treasure hunt.

🐝 Date and Time

Before going to bed, write down the date and your bedtime. Not only will you be able to track your sleeping patterns, but subconsciously you'll also be preparing your journal for a new entry in the morning.

🐝 Write Keywords

Don't worry about writing a novel, you're not getting paid for this. Come morning, you might not want to write down every detail. Feel free to jot down the important moments as bullet points and expand upon them later when you're not a zombie.

🐝 Write in the Present Tense

When expanding on your dreams, write in the present tense as if you're currently experiencing it. For example:

The polar bear is staring me straight in the eye—
he bends down and hands me a cupcake.

Writing and thinking in the present will put your mind back into the dream and allow you to recall more detail.

🐝 Title Your Dreams

After you write your dreams down, go back and give them a title. Pick something that sums up the essence of the trip such as "Midnight Snack with Polar Bear" or "The Joyful Parade." This practice will help later on when you interpret the dream. It'll also help you find old dreams when you're searching for them.

🐝 Notes

Make a note of whether you were lucid or not by putting the word *LUCID* at the top left corner of your entry. Write down what triggered your lucidity, how long it lasted, what you did, and any useful tips you learned that will help with later lucid adventures.

I woke up one morning to find I had written a keyword down: the name of one of my professors from college. Surprised I dreamed about him, I wondered why he was on my mind, since I hadn't spoken to him in over four years. Three days later, I get an email from . . . you guessed it, my professor! Taking this as a direct sign from my dreams to meet with him, I told him about the coincidence of him being in my dreams just days before. We met for coffee and he gave me some very helpful advice—actually on writing this book! If I had been too lazy to write his name down in the middle of the night, I would have forgotten the dream and this experience would not have happened. —THOMAS P.

Finding Meaning Behind Our Dreams

"A dream is an answer to a question we haven't learned to ask." Those words were spoken by Special Agent Dana Scully, the skeptical FBI agent from the *X-Files,* but the concept isn't paranormal. Freud, Jung, and the other founders of modern psychology all insist that dreams mean something. They reveal to us insights about ourselves and our lives. Whether lucid or not, our dreams reflect the inner workings of our psyche and can be highly useful in learning more about ourselves.

By keeping a dream journal you can see things about yourself that you normally dismiss with your everyday waking mind.

Health issues can pop up in our dreams long before we see symptoms in the waking world. Our relationships sneak into the plot of our dreams and reveal our true feelings, both good and bad. Drifting up to the surface are habits we need to look at, patterns we keep repeating, guidance for everyday problems, and beneficial changes we need to make in order to improve our lives. A dream journal records all of this, displaying the buried secrets that our dreams exhume. Think of your dream journal as the SparkNotes to your inner world.

Many of us see dreams as puzzles, little riddles to be solved. We buy dream dictionaries to understand their meaning. Well it's time to throw away your dream dictionary; it'll do more good in the local landfill. The fact is, the dream belongs to the dreamer. Dreams are very personal, intimate things. An apple to us is not an apple to you. An apple to us five years ago is different from our present-day association with an apple. We believe that you and you alone are the final authority on what your dreams mean. What do you think they are saying?

LEARNING FROM OUR DREAMS

Aristotle said that the insights available from dreams were like objects reflected in water. When the water is calm, the forms are easy to see; when the water is agitated (that is, when the mind is emotionally disturbed), the reflections become distorted and meaningless. The more the mind can be still before sleep, said Aristotle, the more the dreamer can learn. If you go to bed calm, the memories of your dreams will be clearer come morning.

Dream Signs, Triggers for Lucid Dreams

As you jot down more of your nighttime adventures, you'll notice that you often dream about very similar things. For example, you might have frequent dreams about your sister, your pet, the ocean, school, snakes—anything. These recurring dream elements are called dream signs, and they're a powerful stepping-stone to lucid dreams. Even now, without knowing it, your dreams contain certain people, events, locations, and situations that pop up again and again, dream after dream.

All too often, my dreams incorporate the idea of home. Sometimes it's my current apartment, other times it's my childhood home, but usually it's some strange blending of all the places I've lived. It is safe to say that my most common dream sign is my place of residence within the dream world. Now, whenever I find myself in "a home" that doesn't pair up with my waking world home, I instantly know that I'm in a dream. —JARED Z.

Once you identify those personal dream signs, they will essentially act as landmarks in the dream world, a great way to achieve lucidity.

Find Your Dream Signs

Keep a journal for a few weeks and you'll begin to see patterns. A dream sign is personal to you. You might have a recurring dream sign that's been with you your whole life, such as fear of snakes. They might change frequently as you yourself change: my new boss. Find a highlighter, read through your dream journal, and start underlining the objects, places, people, and themes that pop up more than once: a large mansion, owls, my brother Joe, the park, embarrassment. Keep a list of all these dream signs.

Locating and identifying dream signs will train your subconscious to spot them the next time they appear. If you recognize that you often dream about your old girlfriend, for example, you can use this as a trigger for becoming aware that you're dreaming. Tell yourself before bed, "The next time I see my ex-girlfriend I will realize that I am dreaming." Knowing that your dreams speak a familiar language with recurring places, people, or themes will be one of the easiest ways to recognize that you're dreaming.

Discovering a Natural World

In January 1832, the HMS *Beagle* drifted through the Atlantic, meandering around volcanic islands, until it finally docked in the archipelago of Cape Verde, off the west coast of Africa. Its passengers stepped onto the rocky islands and began examining and cataloging its natural life. Charles Darwin, a young man of twenty-three, walked along the shore. He wrote about one of his findings that day, an octopus that changed colors like a chameleon. He must have stared at it with awe as the creature's flesh transformed from yellow to green to red.

If writing down your dreams feels like a chore, try to shift your approach. Imagine that you are crafting a book of tales from a completely different dimension, the log of a pioneer, because in essence, that is exactly what you are doing. You are an explorer, and the uncharted terrain is your own inner universe.

As your dream journal grows, so will your relationship with your dreams. You'll soon be dreaming more, having longer and richer dreams, and a wonderful list of common themes and symbols will start to take shape. Hey, you may even learn a thing or two about yourself along the way.

Summary

- Writing down your dreams is the most effective way to remember them.

- Dreams contain insights that we often miss unless we write them down and then go back and reread them.

- Dream signs are essentially recurring elements of your dreams and are a perfect way to recognize the dream state.

- Jot down important points as soon as you wake up, otherwise you might forget.

- Have fun with your dream journal. It's a book of your experiences from another dimension.

The Reality Check

Reality is frequently inaccurate.

—Douglas Adams,
writer, humorist, defender of the black rhino

How do you know that this isn't a dream? You might say, "Well of course I'm awake, I can see a world around me, smell things, touch and taste the external world. I'm sitting here reading this book, dammit!" This is good evidence, but we're afraid it's not enough. If you were in a dream right now, it'd feel just as real. All that clever evidence you had—sight, touch, taste, smell, sound—all that exists in the dream world too. The multisensory experience, the authenticity of emotions, the solidity of our surroundings—all these elements are so convincing that it doesn't occur to our brain that we're in a dream. This is why recognizing the dream state takes an inquisitive mind. This chapter is about training your mind to be inquisitive.

> I'm in a body of water, and I'm following this little cartoon guy as he swims through the water. I want to continue following him under the water, and I think to myself, I can breathe underwater in dreams. I abandon the snorkel and continue following the little cartoon guy. —AMY B.

So stop for a moment right now and look around you, really check this time. Is it possible that you're dreaming? Test it to make sure. Can you push your finger through your hand? Can you pass through a solid object? If you jump, do you float down?

By asking this question, you're performing what is called a reality check, and the beauty of it is this: By asking yourself the question "Am I dreaming?" throughout your day, you will begin to ask the same question while in a dream. Your suspicion of reality

> For two days, I asked myself as many times as I could remember, whether or not I was dreaming. Of course almost every time I was not, and it felt weird to continue asking, but I did like how it brought me more presence and awareness in my waking state. On the second night, I found myself outside of my house and I stopped to ask the same question, "Am I dreaming?" I tested by looking at my hands. Much to my surprise, when I counted my fingers I saw that I had eleven fingers. I checked again. "I am dreaming!" I shouted. It was the best feeling to have finally answered the question with a "YES! This is a dream!" I ran and jumped into flight, testing my Superman skills. —DAVID G.

will echo into your sleep, bouncing around your mind until—voilà!—you find yourself in the mecca of your own psyche. Reality checks are another cornerstone of lucid dreaming.

If you stop and think about it, you can usually tell if you're dreaming or not: The trick is stopping and thinking about it. It may sound crazy to ask this question when you know for sure that you're awake, but your feelings of lunacy will be justified when you have your first lucid dream. Soon enough you'll perform a reality check in a dream and realize: "Wait a second, it worked! I am dreaming!" This sudden realization will be so amazing that it will validate all of your efforts to practice during the waking state.

Physical Test

In order to perform a reality check you not only need to ask the question "Am I dreaming?" but you also have to answer it. And how do you answer your own question, since the dream state likes to trick us and disguise itself as "real"? Fortunately, over the years the lucid dreaming community has developed some clever double checks. Make sure to always perform a physical test as well. Some standard physical tests are:

🐝 **The Finger.** Can you pass your finger through the palm of your hand? In a dream this is possible.

🐝 **The Hand.** Do your hands look normal? Do they have as many fingers as they're supposed to have?

🐝 **The Jump.** Jumping is not only a hell of a lotta fun but a great reality check. If you jump, do you float down, is there an absence of gravity? In dreams floating is absolutely possible. (As a stepping-stone, try floating before you try to fly!)

🐝 **The Nose.** When you hold your nose, can you still breathe? Most lucid dreamers find this to be the most reliable evidence that they're dreaming.

🐝 **The Mirror.** Does your reflection look normal?

🐝 **Reading.** Can you read the same sentence twice without it changing? Can you read the same sentence twice without it *chulnging?*

> Twice within the last year I performed a test within a dream—once I tried to fly to test whether it was a dream. I could not fly and decided it was real. Whoops! Next time I tried to make my hand turn purple. I concentrated hard within the dream and it worked! I was excited to know it was a dream but thought, "Now what?" and the dream ended. —SUSAN D.

As you can see by Susan's example, a second physical test might be necessary; sometimes your first test doesn't work, fooling you into thinking that you are awake when really you're in a dream.

When to Perform a Reality Check

If you ask yourself throughout the day the golden question, it will eventually trickle into your dreams. This is why the reality check is one of the easiest and most rewarding techniques you can try. The question is easy to ask, but turning it into a habit can be a bit challenging for some. Try it out for the next three days, five to ten times a day. Take on this simple habit for even a short period of time—it can spark your first lucid dream. If you need help reminding yourself to do the check, here are some helpful habit-creating tips:

1. **Set an alarm** on your cell phone every hour or two as a reminder to perform a reality check.

I was in my room standing near my bed. It was still dark out and I thought to myself, "How did I get to be standing up? Did I get up to go to the bathroom?" Thinking that there's no way I could be dreaming, I tested just to make sure by jumping. My hands passed right through the ceiling of my apartment! "Whoa, good thing I checked!" I remember thinking. Now fully aware that I'm dreaming, I passed the rest of my body through the ceiling and began walking around in the apartment above me. Seeing nothing of interest, I went outside and began exploring. —THOMAS P.

2. Perform a reality check (choose one or two):
   • Every time you answer your phone.
   • Every time you walk through a doorway.
   • Every time you see a dog.
   • After every meal.
   • Every time you change locations.
   • When something strange happens.
   • Every time you hear music.
   • Every time you smell something delicious.
   • When you're in an emotionally engaging situation.

3. Use dream signs. Remember those recurring symbols from your dreams, the dream signs that popped up in your journal? Here's where they come in handy. Perform a reality check every time you see a dream sign in waking life. If, for example, a dog appears often in your dreams, when you see a dog at any point, stop for

a moment and do a reality check. Am I dreaming? If you often dream about a friend or a sibling, practice for the next three days by doing a reality check every time you see or think of them. Since these are the recurring symbols of your dreams, it's very likely that you'll spot a dream sign while in the dream world, perform a reality check, and become lucid.

Becoming Present

Like the "check engine" light on your car's dashboard, reality checks will alert you when something is out of the ordinary. By asking the question during your waking hours, not only will the practice carry over into your dreams, but it will also have a powerful effect on your waking awareness. By taking a moment and observing the world around you, you will be brought into the moment, be more present, and increase your self-awareness. Much of our days is filled with a constant jabbering going on in our heads. A reality check is a great way to take us out of zombie mode, allowing us to achieve an expanded awareness throughout our daily lives. Use it as an opportunity to come back to the present moment, look around, and see the nice things that surround you. The waking world can be a real trip too.

TOTEM

Keep a small item that is personal to you in your pocket, on your key chain, or somewhere you'll see it throughout your day. Whenever you see it, or feel it in your pocket, perform a reality check. This will help you create the habit of determining if you're dreaming or not, which will then carry over into your dreams.

Summary

You begin your dialogue with the dream world while you are awake, with reality checks.

- By asking yourself throughout your day "Am I dreaming?" you will soon ask the same question while in a dream. "Yes! I am dreaming this time!"

- As you pose the question, perform a physical check as well.

- Perform a reality check five to ten times a day, at regular intervals. Use a consistent occurrence to remind yourself to perform a reality check, such as "every time you see a dog."

PART THREE

ARRIVAL

Now that you've packed your bags, it's time to get going. Your destination is not always the easiest place to find, but we'll guide you through your arrival. Pretty soon you'll look around and take in the strange but familiar surroundings.

As we were learning how to lucid dream, we came to realize that becoming lucid wasn't an impossible skill, as some people might think. After trying out various techniques, it seemed just as accessible as any hobby or sport: We simply trained our bodies and minds to form new habits.

Being disciplined was important, but we discovered that the right frame of mind was even more essential. So be confident, upbeat, and willing to fail in order to try again. The wrong state of mind is like a Chinese finger trap: The more you force it, the more frustration and pressure you exert, the less likely you'll have a lucid dream. If you stay focused and relaxed, the dream will simply come to you.

Can you feel the excitement? We're almost there! After this section you'll have all the knowledge you need to enter a world of your own creation. Have fun. We'll see you on the other side.

Becoming Lucid

In forming a bridge between body and mind, dreams may be used as a springboard from which man can leap to new realms of experience lying outside his normal state of consciousness.

—Ann Faraday,
dream writer, advocate for personal dream interpretation

On July 20, 1969, a machine with legs like a spider detached from the command module and touched down on the surface of the moon. If they had been able to survive without their helmets on, the astronauts would have heard the complete silence of outer space. Commander Neil Armstrong's foot reached the surface, but because of the constraint of the suit he was wearing, he was not able to see the historic footprint that he made. He described the surface as having a powdery feel. Buzz Aldrin joined him, looking out at the empty landscape, finding that double kangaroo jumps were the most effective way to get around.

Hundreds of thousands of miles away, the Earth listened to the men speak. In an attempt to describe this strange place, Aldrin used the phrase "magnificent desolation."

If you've ever wanted to reach out into the mystery of outer space yourself, lucid dreaming is not far off. In this chapter we'll finally arrive in our dreams, using the tools we've collected over the last few chapters. Houston, we're about to touch down.

The word *typical* is nowhere close to describing the profound experience of being conscious in the dream state, but there is a typical way to become lucid. In fact, an average 72 percent of lucid dreams tend to happen in this way, with a technique the lucid dreaming community calls a DILD or a "Dream-Initiated Lucid Dream." A DILD is simply a dream where you become lucid after the dream has already started.

The spontaneous lucidity of this technique usually stems from some sort of trigger: an inconsistency, a dream sign, anything that makes the dreamer stop and question "Am I dreaming?" while in the dream. This chapter will focus on this method, as we've found it to be the easiest way to experience lucidity.

If you've set an intention before bed, performed reality checks throughout your day, or trained yourself to recognize dream signs, perhaps you've become lucid already. These waking world techniques will be helpful in this chapter, and we'll crank it up a notch by adding another killer technique to the mix. Just like Aldrin and Armstrong, soon enough you'll be taking your first steps onto a strange terrain.

The Problem

R emember Rapid Eye Movement (REM), that stage of sleep where your brain is completely active yet your body is asleep, the time in which we dream? To learn lucid dreaming this stage is incredibly important. The goal is to direct all your energy at REM, to focus your intention on those open windows of time when you're actually dreaming.

Here's the problem.

When we set an intention before bed, we don't hit a substantial period of REM for nearly an hour after falling asleep. There are three stages of sleep you go through before even getting to REM. Your intention has to wait in line for light sleep and deep sleep to pass by before it gets its chance to shine.

Often enough, as we enter REM, we've forgotten our original plan: to have a lucid dream. Your goals to see a dream sign or to perform a reality check will continue to fade as you progress through additional sleep cycles.

If only there were some clever, simple solution to this problem, a way to go to sleep right into a dream, bypassing the amnesia of deep sleep! Don't panic, there is a way.

Wake-Back-to-Bed

T he last two windows of REM occur at the end of our sleep cycles, in the early morning hours. Although we dream on and off throughout the night, lucid dreamers tend to focus on these last two stages for a couple of reasons:

They're the longest. As the night progresses, the amount of time you spend dreaming increases. The last two stages of REM are the longest—nearly fifty minutes each—giving you a great chance to have long, vivid, conscious dreams.

No more deep sleep. Since you've already gotten your deep sleep over with earlier in the night, the only thing that lies between the last two stages of REM is a small sliver of light sleep. Your body is still tired, but your mind is primed for dreaming.

Easier to remember. Subjects waking up directly out of a dream have better dream recall. Focus on these last two stages of sleep and it's likely that you'll remember your lucid dreams directly after waking.

Armed with this knowledge, let's trick Mother Nature by catching our last two REM cycles. This feat is done with a technique known as wake-back-to-bed. Simply put, it involves waking up after six hours of sleep, staying awake for twenty minutes, then going back to bed. This thrifty solution sends you back to bed right before you enter the last windows of REM.

> The first lucid dream I had was spontaneous. It was one of the most memorable moments of my life. I was camping at the time and had spent the day by my tent reading a book. I had felt quite meditative all day, but other than that I had not tried any technique either during the day or as I was falling asleep, it just happened out of the blue at about 4:00 a.m. Like I said, it was one of the most amazing experiences I ever had, waking up in a "dream world" being fully awake in that world, spinning and jumping around in excitement, unbelievable excitement. —JACK G.

How to Catch Your Last REM Cycle

By waking up just before your last REM cycles begin, you're essentially putting your sleep on "pause." When you go back to bed twenty minutes later, you'll be diving right into a nice, refreshing swimming pool of your own dreams. With wake-back-to-bed, setting an intention, looking for dream signs, and focusing on becoming aware in your dreams become very effective. Here is the step-by-step technique:

Step 1: Set Your Alarm for Six Hours After Bedtime

Wake up around six hours after you go to sleep. This tends to be a reliable number, but results may vary. If your early morning wake-up time isn't working, try variations. For example, if you're sleeping for a total of eight hours, maybe you'd want to try to catch the very last REM cycle, so you'd want to set your alarm for seven hours after your bedtime, not six. If you have difficulty returning to sleep after a wake-back-to-bed, stick with six hours; it will be easier to fall back asleep with this option.

Step 2: Wake Up for Twenty Minutes

Wake up and stay up for around fifteen to twenty minutes. Staying awake for this span of time awakens your left brain, the analytical half of your mind, which is essential for realizing that "Whoa, this is a dream!" Without your active left brain there to help, your creative right brain will happily get carried away in the whimsy of the dream. In other words, you don't want to simply wake up for a few seconds and fall back to sleep. We know, your bed looks so

cozy you could just cry. But this technique is basically pointless unless you stay up, get your brain thinking clearly and logically, and then go back to bed with a strong intention.

Step 3: Go Back to Bed

Now you can get back into bed and ooze into a state of comfortable relaxation. Many have found that sleeping on your back helps with lucid dreaming, so we recommend that you try this position. As you fall back to sleep, you want to focus your mind on your intention: "I will realize that I'm dreaming."

Step 4: Affirm It

Tell yourself over and over "I am aware that I'm dreaming." Let this be your dominant thought as you fall asleep.

Step 5: See It

Behind your closed eyelids, visualize yourself inside a dream. See yourself becoming lucid and realizing that you're dreaming. See yourself noticing a dream sign or doing a reality check. Imagine it with all of your five senses. The stronger the visualization the better.

Step 6: Feel It

Feel the excitement and emotions that come with being lucid in a dream, when you stop and perform a reality check only to realize that you are in fact dreaming. Feel the incredible freedom of being aware—without boundaries or limits—inside a dream.

Step 7: Expect It

As you repeat the phrase "I am aware that I'm dreaming," you will begin sinking into sleep. Remember, you're not simply turning off like a robot, you're an explorer on a journey to your own inner universe. An incredible adventure awaits you. The next place you'll find yourself in will be a dream.

THINGS TO DO IN THE FIFTEEN TO TWENTY MINUTES WHILE AWAKE

• Read past dreams from your dream journal.

• Look over your list of dream signs.

• Read this book (or another book about lucid dreaming if you must).

• Take a pee.

• Draw a picture of a dream you'd like to have.

• Get up and walk around.

• Write a letter to your subconscious.

• Continuously ask yourself "Am I dreaming?" until you go back to sleep.

Eureka! You're In.

Welcome to Wonderland! You're Alice and you just hit the floor of the rabbit hole. The moment that you recognize that you're dreaming will be an exciting one, so give yourself a big pat on the back for this accomplishment. If this is your first lucid dream, then it's likely you now know what all the fuss is about. The experience is profound—you've just discovered a completely uncharted terrain.

CAT NAP

Naps can be a really effective way to perform a wake-back-to-bed as well. During naps, our bodies are tired but our minds are relatively more awake than in normal sleep. Some nappers fall right into REM or start dreaming soon after they fall asleep, so your chances of a lucid dream are pretty good. Much more research needs to be done in this area, but experts suggest to nap for twenty minutes, forty minutes, or ninety minutes.

Quite often, the amateur lucid dreamer's early exploits in lucidity last only a few moments. If you've become lucid already but lost your awareness very quickly, don't worry. This is common. In the next chapter we'll look at ways in which you can stabilize the dream and stay lucid for long stretches of time. And if you haven't become lucid yet, do not fret. There's plenty of time to practice.

After Aldrin and Armstrong's lunar module landed, they were supposed to sleep for five hours before leaving the cabin and venturing out onto the surface of the moon—they'd been awake for a while after all. The astronauts ignored this plan and left as soon as possible. They were just too excited to sleep. Wouldn't you be? Charles Conrad Jr. was the third man to step on the moon. "Whoopee!" he said. "Man, that may have been a small one for Neil, but that's a long one for me!" We know just how he feels.

Summary

- The most common way to have a lucid dream is to become aware during a regular dream.

- The most effective way to accomplish this involves performing the waking techniques that trigger awareness, such as reality checks, finding dream signs, and setting intentions to become lucid before bed.

- To maximize results, catch the last (or second to last) REM cycle by waking up six hours after you go to sleep and then going back to bed.

- Before going back to bed, stay up for fifteen to twenty minutes and get your brain active. Go to sleep with the intention of becoming lucid, seeing a dream sign, or performing a reality check.

Staying Lucid

I soon realized that no journey carries one far unless, as it extends into the world around us, it goes an equal distance into the world within.

—Lillian Smith,
author, social critic, and notorious fighter for equal rights

The small boat bobs in the ocean, thrown around by waves. You jump off the lip of the boat and hit the water. With a kick of your flipper, you find yourself engulfed by the blue ocean. The protective casing of your scuba mask grants you sights of exotic coral and fish. Ten seconds go by, and normally that'd mean time to surface; that small breath of oxygen in your lungs would be depleting. But fortunately, there's an O_2 tank strapped to your back and a hose leading to your mouth. As a scuba diver, you can swim underneath the waves for a long while without worry. A pink cloud floats by, tiny speckles of plankton, and you swim. You're free to search for strange fish, crustaceans, and whales. You've got all the time in the world.

Most lucid dreamers would agree: There's nothing more frustrating than getting lucid and losing your awareness shortly thereafter.

As lucid dreamer Dominic O. explains, "It felt like I had woken up and I immediately decided to start messing with things. I acted out my fantasies of doing and saying whatever I want, but holding on to that awareness was too difficult to last more than a few minutes in the dream. Instead of lapsing back into being unlucid, I woke up."

Whether you wake yourself up out of excitement or sink back into an unconscious dream, awareness doesn't always stick once you find it. It requires a delicate balance. The ability to remain lucid is a skill that every lucid dreamer must learn if they want to explore the dream world.

We know it can be exciting. Throughout the day you ask yourself, "Am I dreaming?" with an obvious "No." The moment the answer becomes an astounding "YES!" you feel a tremendous rush of emotions. This excitement causes many beginners to wake themselves up, back in their bedroom again. No need to feel bad about it. It happens to the best of us, and there's always tomorrow night.

For other dreamers, the problem may be more subtle. In the waking world, we might get so engrossed in a TV show that we forget about the popcorn that's been in the microwave for fifteen minutes. A similar bad habit often occurs when you're lucid. Getting lost in whatever dream activity you're doing can be consuming and before you know it, you're back to having a regular ol' dream. In order to master lucid dreaming, you must stay balanced with one foot in the dream and one foot out. In other words, engage the dream but never forget that you're dreaming.

To hold on to that self-awareness, get in the habit of anchoring yourself in the dream. To anchor, simply stop what you're doing and perform a technique that sharpens your focus. The result is a stable dream environment that you can explore freely and for longer periods of time. Learning how to prolong your lucidity is like having a tank of oxygen when diving. With it, you can explore the ocean for much longer. Instead of skimming the surface, your tank allows you to travel deep into the sea, down to the ocean floor where the real treasures of your subconscious are hiding.

When to Anchor Your Dream

1. **Upon becoming lucid.** The first moments of a lucid dream are the most crucial, so perform these stabilizing techniques directly after becoming lucid. Before jumping into your dream adventure, always pause for a second and anchor yourself in the dream by performing the techniques that follow in this chapter. If you're too hasty, you won't go very far anyhow.

2. **When the dream starts fading.** When the lucid dream is in danger of becoming a normal dream again, you'll actually see it happen. As your lucid dreaming abilities progress, you'll notice that the first of your five senses to go is often sight. Visual elements begin to fade and corrode. As if you stood up too quickly from a chair, the world in front of you will blur and darken. We have a big, fancy, incredibly hard-to-pronounce word for this phenomenon: fading. If the dream begins getting fuzzy or lacks richness, you'll know you're fading and that it's time to stabilize.

3. To amp up lucidity. Most important, these techniques will allow you to heighten your level of awareness. Even if your lucid dream isn't at risk of ending, it's possible for your awareness to lessen. Awareness is not a binary switch, on or off. It lies on a spectrum from "zombie" to "Buddha" and everything in between.

Stabilization Techniques

The techniques below work in any of the three situations: whether you've just become lucid, are starting to fade, or want to amp up your awareness. Pick the few that work best for you and have fun mixing and matching various techniques.

Keep Calm and Carry On

Lucidity can be a very powerful and stimulating experience. But like a feral horse, unless you control and tame your excitement it'll get away from you. We know, it's hard to ignore the childlike voice in your head telling you to celebrate. "Wahooo, I'm lucid!"

Put down your flute of champagne and hold off on the celebration until after you wake up. As soon as you get lucid, stay calm and try to relax. Take a deep breath of dream air, look around, and instead of complimenting yourself on being such a whiz, take it slow. Once you're calm you can begin exploring.

Spinning

Try this technique, which was introduced by Stephen LaBerge. He was searching for a way to prolong his lucidity during his research and stumbled upon this highly effective approach. The idea is very

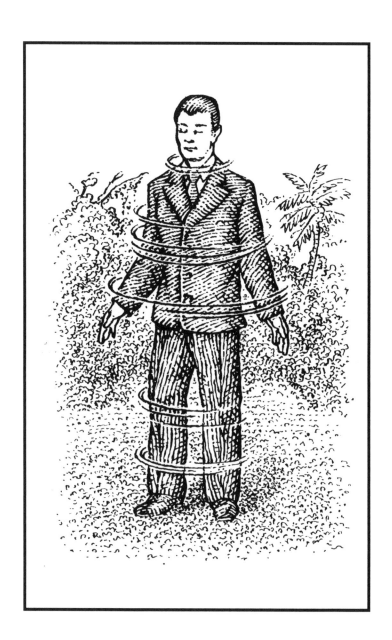

simple. To stabilize the dream, spin yourself (your dream body) around like you're doing a pirouette.

You don't need to be a master ballerina; simply turn yourself in a clockwise or counterclockwise direction. Dr. LaBerge notes that information on balance and movement are closely related with visual information. The sensory experience of spinning will produce a stable picture of the world around you, and it will make it difficult for your mind to communicate with your physical, sleeping body, which could wake you up.

Stay Engaged

You're in a dream—don't just stand there, begin your adventure! The passive dreamer will soon find himself forgetting that he's in a dream. You don't have to go crazy, just find a tactile way to interact with your surroundings. Dr. LaBerge has a lot of experience with this pesky problem and advises us to load our perceptual system so it cannot change its focus from the dream world to the waking world. Because you'll always have them at your disposal, try concentrating on your own hands. Look at them, really examine them. Focus on something and stay active—it will always help to stabilize the dream.

I found myself in my parents' house downstairs. The thought crossed my mind that I must be dreaming, so I tested it out by attempting to fly toward the sliding glass door. I could fly and instantly became lucid. Feeling a bit unstable, I quickly focused my attention on the sliding glass door. I pushed my leg through it and felt the coldness it produced. It was like putting my leg through a streaming waterfall of ice. The sensation intrigued me and I walked around feeling what other things felt like in the dream world. —SAM O. T.

Strike a Balance

While it's important to stay engaged in the dream, don't get too wrapped up in one thing for too long. You might forget that you're in a dream. The goal is to strike a balance between interacting with the dream while at the same time remaining cognizant that it's a dream. The Bible will back us up on this: "Be in the world, but not of it." When it comes to the plot of the dream, try to have one foot in and one foot out, a balance of mindfulness.

Touch Something

Get your head out of the gutter, we're not talking about dream sex (just yet). Engaging any of your five senses, especially the sensation

> I was on a very crowded boat. I became lucid and said to this couple, "We're in a dream right now." She didn't know what I meant. I said, "I got to go, but before I do, I'm going to show you that you're also dreaming. What would it take to prove that to you? If I flew right now, would that show you that we're in a dream?" She said, "Yeah." The dream started visually fading so I first spun and then repeated "stabilize" twice. I was back to being grounded, and the dream assumed its richness again. I flew up and hovered beside the boat. I remember that the woman was very surprised. I also remember floating to the upper deck and making eye contact with another woman. I made a face like "Yeah, I'm flying . . ." as if I was so cool. She wasn't impressed and rolled her eyes. —NICOLAS L.

of touch, will help stabilize the dream world. Try a technique called the finger touch. Touch each of your fingers to your thumb and concentrate, feeling your dream body. Touch a wall, a plant, or the ground. Rub your hands together. Pick something up and feel the weight of it. Concentrate on other senses, such as hearing and taste. The main idea here is to stimulate your focus.

The more you can focus, the better (on a sensation, the dream world, or on your dream body). No matter how hard the ocean tugs at your ship, your awareness will remain steady with this anchor.

Command the Dream

If you're midflight, it might be hard to rub your hands together or touch something—especially if your flight style resembles Superman—so here's an approach that can be used anytime, anywhere. Simply command the dream verbally by saying something out loud that will help your focus. Actually speaking (sometimes shouting) the word "stabilize!" or "clarity!" or "increase lucidity" will serve as a reminder to both your conscious and your subconscious that your intention is to focus. Don't be shy, use this technique frequently throughout the dream. Whenever you begin to feel the dream fading, command it to stabilize. The results are usually immediate.

Meditate

Want to blow your mind? This final technique allows the dreamer to raise his or her awareness to a much higher level. This approach isn't recommended for beginners but there's no harm in trying. If lucidity is a spectrum, then using this technique will send you off the charts. It requires the dreamer to sit and meditate while lucid in the dream. That's right. The practice of meditation works the same in the dream world as it does in the waking world. Sit down and concentrate on your breath and focus on the sounds around you. Continuously remind yourself of the realization that you are dreaming. Notice any sounds or sensations? Is there a breeze blowing in your dream? Can you hear birds, or children, or traffic? Feel how solid the ground is, yet understand that this is not "real"? Develop the mind-

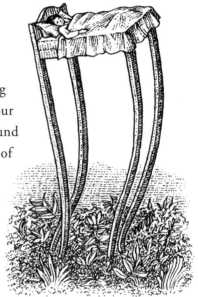

fulness that you are in your own subconscious and that whatever appears out there is really a reflection of you.

DREAM REENTRY

You know how video games let you "continue" after you've lost? If you accidentally wake up from your lucid dream, don't worry, all hope is not lost. Lie there and don't move or open your eyes. Focus back on the dream, especially the location and setting of the dream. Remember the details as you drift back to sleep, reminding yourself, "I'm dreaming . . . I'm dreaming . . ." It's likely you'll find yourself back in the same lucid dream, as if you never left. Three . . . two . . . one . . .

Levels of Lucidity

In the dream world there are various levels of lucidity. You might realize you're dreaming but that somehow everything is not in your control. You might have a vague awareness that you're dreaming but are unable to direct your own actions in the dream. Or you might have very high awareness—you are the creator of, and at one with, everything around you. The levels of awareness lie on a spectrum. Here is a basic reference to these levels:

LEVEL ONE. No awareness whatsoever. You dreamed but have no recollection of it. In other words, you were dreaming unconsciously.

LEVEL TWO. Slight awareness that you're dreaming and are able to act or make decisions. Dream recall is easier.

LEVEL THREE. You know that you're dreaming but see things "out there" as separate from you. You have a hard time influencing the dream environment.

LEVEL FOUR. You know that you're dreaming and that everything "out there" is really "in here"; there is no separation. Mastery over dream elements and creation.

LEVEL FIVE. The very end, or is it? This level is known only to masters of the dream state. It goes beyond the normal interactions with the dream world. The projections of the dream world dissolve and you reach a level of pure conscious awareness.

Now That You're Anchored

The sea can be rough out there. No matter your skill level, the know-how to stabilize a lucid dream will always come in handy. Practice using a few of these techniques by themselves or in combination with one another. As you learn how to prolong your lucidity, you're getting familiar with the dream world, how it feels and behaves. With the valuable gift of time, you can walk around, talk to dream characters, and deliberately seek out and ask questions to the dream. Your skills will increase and your lucidity will last for longer and longer periods of time.

Your tank is strapped on, your gear in place, you've got a full tank of oxygen. All right, Cousteau, the next part of the adventure is up to you. Let's take a look at the best ways to explore this mysterious place.

Summary

- Staying aware once you're lucid requires a delicate balance of mindfulness.

- To prolong your lucidity, try anchoring yourself within the dream by performing techniques that will sharpen your focus and that constantly remind you that you're dreaming.

- Performing these techniques will help you create a stable dream environment, a solid landscape that you can explore and traverse just like the physical world.

PART FOUR

EXPLORING A NEW WORLD

Y ou have made it through the brush. If you haven't already become conscious in your dreams, you will soon enough. Lucid or not, the adventure is far from over. In fact, it's just beginning. The journey is just like a classic myth, a knight-in-shining-armor story, or a tall tale. It will take you face-to-face with yourself, leading toward an understanding of who you really are and what's possible. The path you're on runs parallel with the waking world.

The following chapters will guide you through some essential information you need to know about the dream world. Here, things are a little peculiar. The rules and principles of the dream world are slightly different from those you're used to. You'll find that you have the ability to fly, to walk through solid objects, to transcend both space and time, to conjure people out of thin air, and to create buildings or even cities. To do these things, you must learn how to speak the language of the dream, how to move around within it, how to influence your surroundings and create with your mind's eye.

From here on out, lucid dreaming will become a whole lot easier for you. As you spend more time in the dream world, your abilities will expand. The tips in this section will be essential in developing your skills as a lucid dreamer.

11

Transportation

When once you have tasted flight, you will forever walk the earth with your eyes turned skyward, for there you have been, and there you will always long to return.

—Leonardo da Vinci,
Renaissance polymath, genius, and cheeky fellow

Miles ahead, mountains loom like the backs of camels under white clouds. You rise to the level of the clouds and air rushes past you as the mountains get closer. Flying over them with ease, you gain speed in the clear, warm air.

Adventure is about the journey, about getting from point A to point B and seeing what you discover along the way. Often it's not the destination that's as important as the voyage you took to get there. As you venture into the dream world, you'll begin to familiarize yourself with the principles of travel and how movement works in dreams. Transportation is one of the most useful and practical abilities in the dream and is a must for any lucid dreamer who wants to explore his or her inner landscape.

Movement in the dream world is a bit different from moving around the waking world. If you want to get somewhere in the waking world, you're used to certain forms of travel: a bus, car, bicycle, skipping, frolicking, just plain walking, etc. You have to move your body, and every movement takes a certain amount of time.

Your morning commute takes forty-five minutes. That relaxing trip to the Bahamas requires you to spend hours on an airplane, trapped next to a crying baby.

In the dream world, this is not the case. The laws of space and time don't apply to the lucid dreamer. Getting from point A to point B is a matter of intention and focus; changes in location can happen instantaneously. With this mastery comes the freedom to explore and travel to far-off places or even distant times.

In this chapter you'll learn some of the easiest ways to travel. Of course there's everyone's favorite—flying. We'll also learn to use doors and mirrors to enter new locations and eliminate movement altogether through teleportation. As a conscious dreamer, you'll no longer be confined to the current dream you are having. You'll be able to use these techniques to explore any place of your choosing.

Want to go to Egypt and see the pyramids? Want to visit your friend's house across the country? Maybe take a quick hop to outer space? No problem. Your suitcases and suntan lotion aren't necessary; all you'll need is a strong intention. Save the gas money and the frequent-flier miles because this trip is completely free.

Transportation Principles

1. **No gravity.** That isn't to say that things are floating around as they would in outer space, but gravity in the dream world is not something that you must abide by. The law of gravity can be broken and bent at will. Soaring through the skies like Wonder Woman, jumping hundreds of feet in the air, or barrel-rolling above moonlit clouds will soon become commonplace.

2. **No space or time.** In the dream world, everything exists in one big eternal now. This notion might seem a bit crazy for us rational thinkers who see time as something that only moves forward, but dream time can be warped or reversed. Travel across great distances in the blink of an eye; nothing is stopping you. You will soon find out just how boundless and infinite this place can be.

3. **Movement via will.** Since you are no longer in a physical space, but rather a "mental"

I start off at a moderate jog. After about two dozen steps, I lift my legs up and float only feet from the ground. I arch my back and aim my head for the pillowlike clouds above me. Slowly, I begin to rise, gaining height with each passing moment. After about fifty yards, I'm soaring with ease right above the trees. I tell myself that I'm in the present moment. The world is real. The sun shines more beautiful than I have ever seen. I can feel its warmth, and it casts gorgeous rays upon the leaves, my hands, and everything in my sight. I stay at a low altitude so that I can glide gleefully at the tops of the trees. I run my fingers through the leaves. Soon Tom joins me. We take off into the clouds, which have already begun turning into giant pillows. —JARED Z.

space, movement (putting one foot in front of the other, also known as walking) is not necessary for travel. As we have just found out, space is not a factor, so moving or traveling requires only one thing: a focused thought or intention. If you want to go somewhere specific, all it will take is your willpower; the scene will change instantaneously.

Lucid in the Sky with Diamonds

It isn't a surprise that flying is the primary form of travel among dreamers. Most people report that this is their favorite thing to do when they find themselves self-aware in their dreams. The feeling of the wind rushing across your face, the freedom and exhilaration of moving in any direction, free of all limitations, is quite an intoxicating experience. Although flying is one of the easiest ways to travel while dreaming, it is a skill that takes confidence and practice to master. You don't have to be an angel to earn your "wings," but developing a capacity to fly with control takes trial and error and a bit of practice.

Think of the following as a flight manual in Aerial Oneironautics. It will teach you the basics needed for dream air travel. As you develop more control, you'll gain new skills and maneuverability. You'll find yourself flying at incredible speeds or at unreachable heights, performing aerial acrobatics that'll make any superhero green with envy.

> When I first began lucid dreaming, I was surprised that flying had to be learned. As if I was walking for the first time, flying had its own intricacies and nuances that made it a unique experience to fully understand. I remember having a very difficult time, for example, on stopping or making sharp turns because I would always fly too fast. I also would have to run for a little while and leap into flight. Taking off without a boost of momentum was tough. I also woke myself up plenty of times because hitting something or flying too fast would jolt me awake. —THOMAS P.

Takeoff

When you become lucid, take a second and ground yourself with some stabilizing techniques before jumping right into flight. It's important to begin your flying modestly. Take it slow, Top Gun. Start off by jumping up and floating. Feel what it's like to be weightless. As you'll quickly find out, gravity only exists in the dream world if we want it to exist. At first it will seem as if gravity and other physical laws are present, but as soon as you focus on drifting up toward the sky you'll see your toes gently lift off the ground. Think "float" and see yourself floating. That's all it takes, it's that easy.

If you still need help getting off the ground, use one of the visualizations below; images of wings or devices will help your logical mind accept the "impossible" reality of flying. These visualizations are, of course, unnecessary, but they can serve as "training wheels" for first-time fliers.

Remember, it's all about your thoughts and expectations. Believe that you can fly and you can, fear that you'll fall and you will. Like Peter Pan and Wendy, think happy thoughts. Each dreamer flies in his or her own method of flight, but here are a few examples. Try a few of them out and see which works best for you.

THE SUPERMAN. Fist forward, just like the Man of Steel.

THE SWIMMER. Swim through the air using a stroke you're comfortable with.

THE OWL. Flap your arms like a bird.

THE SCI-FI/FANTASY. Use a helpful device such as a jet pack or magic carpet.

THE BOUNCE. Take leaps and progressively jump higher each time. Tell yourself that you are weightless. On the last jump, lean forward, and jump into the flight.

THE PIXIE. Shape-shift into a bird or grow butterfly wings.

Speed

You jump into flight and start gaining altitude. The ground below you shrinks, and your body moves faster, lurching forward toward the horizon.

Now that you're up in the air, there's the matter of control. Flight can easily get unstable and out of balance. If you're flying too fast, making a sharp turn can be quite the difficult maneuver. Controlling your speed and ability to turn is an important step in your flight training. When starting off, keep your speed to a nice cruise so that you can get used to the feeling and weight of your dream body. Venture one hundred feet into the air. Come back down and do it again. Think of slowing down, and you'll slow down. Think of going faster, and you'll soar. As long as you're in control of your thoughts, the sky is the limit. Well, we take that back, the sky has no limits either.

Agility

As a novice flier, try to avoid turns—a straight flight will require less control and will be much more stable. An erratic flight pattern could cause the dreamer to wake up. When you're confident enough, turning can be easy, as long as it's gradual. Leaning your weight in the desired direction will be sure to pull you into that turn. As with riding a bike, if you want to turn left, simply lean to the left. It's that simple.

Uh-oh, there's a building ahead and you're about to smash into it! If you need to make sharper turns or if you're going really fast, it's always easiest to lead with your head. To turn quickly, stay calm, then turn your head and focus on moving in the new direction. Your body will follow. It's also important to stay active and engaged while lucid. If your head is in the clouds, you may get too caught up in flight and lose awareness altogether. During flight, continue to perform reality checks and stay aware by reminding yourself, "This is a dream, this is a dream!"

Landing

You're soaring four hundred feet above the ground, and it's incredible. Up ahead you see something familiar: your old house. As you lower your altitude, you realize that your speed is not decreasing. You try to cut to the side, but it's too late. Bam! Like a Looney Tunes character you smack right into the building, little bluebirds circling around your head.

Fortunately you can't actually be harmed in dreams, but the shock can definitely wake you up. Sorry to say, there's no flying in the waking world, even if your bed is in the shape of a spaceship. Flying is not only a form of entertainment but a means of getting somewhere specific, so while staying in the air is fun, it's good to know how to land. Landing allows you to continue your adventure without getting carried away with the addictive fun of flight.

How to Land

1. Think of a place where you want to go. Knowing where you want to go next will ensure that you are actively engaging the dream; the risk of fading is lowered.

2. Descend slowly at the angle an airplane would.

3. Lean back like you're pulling on the reins of a horse. Pull your weight back and try to float into a nice speed for landing.

4. Hit the ground as softly as possible, moving your feet like you're walking.

> I look up at the stars and take off. I could have just teleported, sure, but I didn't trust my ability to teleport at the time. The stars and galaxies shoot by me like bullets until I decide I'm there. I see a planet approach and I land on it, finding myself surrounded by snow and lights. —MARK R. W.

5. Go explore! You didn't come here for nothing.

Flying doesn't have to be limited to Earth. In dreams, outer space has plenty of oxygen, and the temperature is quite nice. Take a tour around the solar system, barrel-roll above the moon, venture into the darkness of space. Who knows what you might find out there?

Other Methods of Travel

F lying may be the most exhilarating form of dream travel, but sometimes it's not the most efficient. Lucid dreams don't last forever, so you may be looking to save a little time, to arrive at your destination before the alarm sounds. Since the dream world is malleable, it's possible to manipulate space in order to expedite your travels. Want to go somewhere specific? Skip the red-eye flight and choose a form below of instantaneous travel.

> I'm in Times Square with some kid. I'm in the middle of teaching him how to fly when I realize that we are dreaming. I tell him to look directly into my eyes. His eyes were weird—like the pupil was misshapen. I try to connect with him. "This is a dream," I say and fly up on top of a large advertisement. The kid mirrors me exactly, and flies with me to the top of the billboard. —GARY P.

Gateways

A nything can be a gateway to another location in a dream. Doors, caves, walls, mirrors—a friend of ours even imagines a giant tube to get to new places (think Mario Bros.). These objects are simply visuals to convince your logical mind that instantaneous travel is possible. Pick a gateway that you feel will work.

Before you step through your desired gateway, set your intention on where you want to go. Even say it out loud to the dream itself: "Take me to the moon." Make sure your intention is passionate by connecting your desired location with an emotion: "I am going to the moon to see the Earth from a distance."

Want to roll the dice? We recommend this option: Let the dream's wisdom guide you to your next destination. When you walk through the gateway, say "Take me where I need to go" and walk on through. There's no telling where you'll end up.

Teleportation

Think it and you're there. Teleportation is like the gateway technique, but without the actual gateway. After all, gateways are just a visualization aid; all you really need to get anywhere is a strong intention.

Remember Le Marquis Saint-Denys, the pioneering nineteenth-century lucid dreamer? He had a trick to get to a new place. He would simply put his dream hands in front of his eyes until the picture went black. He would then intend to be

> I wonder if I can create a portal. I use my right index finger to trace a circle on the mirror-wall. I don't know what exactly made me pick this destination, but in my thoughts, I pick "heaven" as the destination that I want to be on the other side of the portal. When I'm finished drawing the circle, the area inside it doesn't transform into a portal; instead, it swings inward, like a door on a hinge. I go through the doorway. —AMY B.

somewhere else and remove his hands. Sometimes he didn't even have to take his hands away. The new scene would simply appear out of the blackness.

Here are three teleportation tips:

1. **Focus and intention.** You must have your intention muscle fully toned for teleportation to work. Since you don't have any visual aids, your mind must be 100 percent focused on where you want to go. For that reason, teleportation is a fun way to hone your intention skills.

2. **Close your eyes.** Even without a portal to walk through you can still use a little trick to help you out. Try closing your eyes—or cover them like Saint-Denys—saying, "When I open my eyes, I'll be standing at the top of the Empire State Building."

3. **Spin in a circle.** The act of spinning in a dream has many benefits. Find a stable location and begin spinning with your eyes open. Think about what your desired location looks like and feels like. Watch as the colors and shapes begin to blend together. As you slow down, the new location will have formed. Paired with a strong intention, this is one of the best ways to change the dream location.

Walking Through Walls

Now that you're in the landscape of your own mind, it's time to explore a little. Test the environment and touch things, feel their lifelike weight and texture. When it comes to lucid dreaming, one of the simplest but most interesting experiences is walking through solid objects. In the dream world, obstacles only appear to be in your way. A window, a brick wall, a rock face—these things are only illusions, projections from your mind. They are not physical. Objects may feel solid when you touch them, but they feel solid only because you expect them to

> In this lucid dream, I just practiced going through things: glass, wood, and tile. I was curious what each one would feel like. I conjured up a pen and paper in my dream and wrote down my observations. Glass felt like ice. I went through it and stayed in it, my arm penetrating this glass door in front of me. It felt really cold. Wood felt like sand, it was grainy. Then I went through tile, and it felt like chalk. I was amazed at the feeling these "objects" generated when I went through them. I wrote these down in my dream, but unfortunately I couldn't bring back these records.
> —THOMAS P.

feel that way. Think of the object as air, and you will pass through it effortlessly.

Time Travel

In the playground of your subconscious, you can step across the sands of time like you're walking to work. Without the constraints of the space-time continuum a dreamer can travel to any historical era or futuristic landscape he or she desires. People, places, and times can all be accessed. In the same way you can bend space, you can bend time. The dream world is boundless and infinite, and everything is available to you in that one big now.

1. **Incubation.** During your wake-back-to-bed, decide on a particular time and place. Let's say you're a big World War II fan and want to arrive in 1945. Spend the last twenty minutes before you go to bed looking at a picture of the era, such as the Times Square shot of the V-J Day kiss. Find video or music from that period as well. This is all to help support your intentions.

2. **Build yourself a time machine.** If you become lucid and you're not in the time period of your choice, you'll have to travel there. Because our minds are hardwired with "cause and effect," it's handy to use a time machine or portal to get you to your desired time period. Your time machine can be anything from a simple wooden doorframe to a DeLorean DMC-12. It should be something you can relate to, something you believe will do the job. Robert Moss, in his book *Dreamgates,* suggests something more organic than a

machine. Visualize a river, he says, "The River of Time." Wading into its waters will bring you into a scene from another era.

3. Restate affirmation. Before walking through the door, stepping into the river, or starting up your contraption, say your intention out loud. "When I open this door, it will be 1945."

Summary

- Moving around the dream world will enrich your dream adventure: Transportation is practical for getting to places and it also provides an experience in and of itself.

- To help move in the dream, create a way to convince your mind that it's possible to do the impossible: Swim through the air, conjure up a magical door, create a time machine, etc.

- While flying or getting around in the dream, all you really need is a focused thought or intention. Nothing else is really necessary.

- Time, space, and physical objects are just illusions in your dream. Even though your surroundings look real, "reality" can easily be bent.

12

Creation

⌒•⌒

Life isn't about finding yourself. Life is about creating yourself.

—George Bernard Shaw,
Irish literary critic, playwright, and snarky gentleman

I n 1888, there were still a lot of blank spots on the map of the American frontier. It was December eighteenth of that year when two cowboys were riding through the Indian territory of southwest Colorado, looking for stray cattle. They stopped their search for cows when they found something else: an ancient clay city built into a huge cliff, abandoned nearly one thousand years earlier by its inhabitants. In the following months, with the help of a Swedish archaeologist, the cowboys explored and excavated the city. They cataloged this amazing feat of creation, the largest cliff dwelling in North America, now called Mesa Verde. It was still filled with objects and art from an early pueblo society.

Creation is at the core of the human spirit. Throughout time, every individual and society has had the overwhelming urge to create. Whether you're an artist, baker, mason, or just an average joe, everyone is a creator in his own right. Even if you're not finger painting as much as you did when you were six years old, you've still crafted your own life, haven't you?

We're different from other animals in our capacity to create and forge new ideas through our will and imagination. This power has allowed us to shape the world around us, as well as influence our own individual experience. The thoughts and beliefs we have, and the actions that we take, mold the world around us. You'll find that it works the same in the dream world.

Creation Principles

In a lucid dream, you can create anything. Nothing is off-limits—no object, creature, or contraption is out of reach. Your creation can be as large as a mountain or as complicated as a living organism. If you could create the impossible, what would you make? While any act of creation is within reach, this chapter will focus on four techniques: the basics of creation, conjuring up friends or family, dream art, and thinking big.

But before we discuss the step-by-step techniques, there's an important question to consider—how do we create in our dreams? When you find yourself fully self-aware, there are a couple of principles to take note of. First off, the dream world might look like the physical world, but there are key differences. Rules, laws, and customs work a bit differently here.

1. **Thoughts and emotions create your reality.** Your thoughts have a very powerful effect on the dream world. Whatever you think about in the dream directly influences the environment around you. If you're calm, you may find yourself near a placid lake. Anxiety or fear in the dream can result in nightmares. Therefore intention and focused thought are key. By focusing your thoughts on a specific place, object, person, or outcome, you will instantaneously create those circumstances around you. Our subconscious thoughts create every building, prop, and event within the dream.

I THINK THEREFORE I'M SCATTERED

Humans have up to forty to fifty thousand thoughts a day, so if thoughts create our dreams, it's no wonder that our dreams can sometimes be a bit disorganized and erratic, especially if we are unconscious within them. A good intention organizes that clutter like a determined chambermaid.

2. **Expectation effect.** The dream world mirrors your own beliefs and expectations. If you believe you can't fly, you won't be able to. If you expect to find a beautiful lady in the next room over, chances are you will. You can create in the dream using your expectations. By taking control of your expectations, you usually have direct influence over the environment. This isn't always the case, however—sometimes you'll have underlying beliefs or expectations that bubble up and affect the dream world. Even though you've become lucid, you may still find yourself battling nightmares and struggling with obstacles: the dysfunctional children of your subconscious mind.

3. The man in the mirror. Wandering around your lucid dream, you will come to realize how intimately connected you are to the dream environment. Even though things appear to be external (there's a desk over there, a chair, a tree, or a bird, whatever) these things are actually a reflection of your own self. A chair, for example, feels solid and real, but it's still a creation of your mind. Once you sink your teeth into this concept, your relationship with the dream changes dramatically. The air around feels alive and rife with possibilities. Instead of trying to change through the strength of your willpower, you begin effortlessly shifting yourself (your thoughts, emotions, and beliefs) in order to change the "outside" world. In other words, don't change the dream, change yourself.

Basics of Creation

Let's start by creating simple objects. Because our logical brain operates through cause and effect, using tools such as doorways, rooms, potions, or flying devices are all helpful when it comes to creation in the dream world. Creating an object out of thin air might not seem easy at first, so these tips will get you started:

1. **Blueprint.** Have the object that you want to create in your mind's eye. Say the desired object is a baseball bat. Hold the image of the bat in your mind.

2. **What's it like?** That clear picture in your mind is helpful, but it's often not enough to conjure something out of thin air. Make sure you feel it; connect some emotion and sensation to the object. What does a baseball bat feel like? What is its texture, its weight? Imagine it in your hands, and use your senses. Did you play baseball as a kid? Do you remember the first time you connected with the ball? The combination of your thoughts and feelings is an unstoppable creative force.

3. **Now find it.** Is conjuring these items out of thin air too tricky? Your left brain is getting in the way, doubting if such a feat is "possible." Try to trick your mind by looking for it elsewhere. Find a doorway to another room and say, "When I open this door or walk into this room, a giant chocolate bar will be inside" or "There is a giant four-headed horse in my backyard waiting for me." If there are no doors or rooms around, you can close your eyes and intend

for the object to be there when you open them. Remember to hold the image in your mind and expect it to be there.

Meeting Friends

You can find old friends, revisit past relationships, or talk with deceased relatives in your dreams. It's as easy as making a rendezvous for coffee on a Sunday afternoon; the experience will be just as real as if your date were there in front of you.

Who knows if these dream characters are impostors—just your mind's projection of so-and-so—or real people? Either way the encounter could lead to a profound healing experience. The recently heartbroken person can find closure with an ex, widows can find peace with their late husbands, or messages can come from friends who know us best. Let's take a look:

1. **Blueprint**. Again, have the person that you want to meet in your mind's eye. Say it's your dad, who passed on a couple of years ago. Can you bring his image to your attention? It might help to glance at a photograph during a wake-back-to-bed.

2. **Feel their presence**. Attach an emotion to this person; that much should be easy. Close your eyes and imagine him in front of you, and really feel his presence. In the case of your father, what does he look like? Feel like? If he were to walk into the room does he have a special presence about him? We all do, so feel it.

3. Find them at a hot spot. Try looking for them where they're usually found, whether it's your old house, a local bakery he frequented, or the factory where he worked. Make it easier on your left brain by providing a familiar stage to set your play. Use doorways, other rooms, close your eyes, anything to trick your mind into believing that you'll find this person nearby.

Creating Works of Art

In the physical world, art has always existed as a way of expressing the inner workings of the human spirit. Its only limits are those of the creator's imagination and the physical laws of the waking world.

> Hastily I make a chamber in the mesa cliff, with a hidden airhole too small for a person to squeeze in or out. I add a "chimney" hole on top so the air will circulate, and then teleport myself inside. I adjust the stone like punching a pillow. —CHRIS W.

But can't we start up an art project in our dreams? Besides its role as an amazing creative outlet, creating art while lucid dreaming has some "practical" benefits: Some works of art can take months, even years, to create in the waking world, but not in the dream state. You can build a huge, complicated work in mere moments. Lucid dreaming also allows you to experiment with art that could not be physically constructed on the planet Earth. For example, if you're an architect, don't wait for that funding to come through—build your dream building!

1. **Intention.** Wake up before your last REM cycle. Slap yourself on the cheeks, some cold water might help. Now, think about the art that you want to create. After deciding upon your creation, go to sleep with the intention of making it.

2. **The right tools for the job.** Because your stubborn brain is still somewhat tied to the physical world, it will be helpful to use the proper tools that you're used to working with. Once you are lucid, seek out your materials or create them. If you are painting something in the dream space, use paint and a brush on canvas. As time goes on, you'll find that you won't need paint tubes. Eventually, brushes will also become obsolete and you'll be able to paint with only your mind.

3. **Thinking outside the frame.** Part of being an artist and a lucid dreamer is trying out new things. The dream world is at your fingertips, so why paint on just canvas? Try painting a building. Hell, trying painting an entire planet! Don't just sculpt a statue, sculpt a civilization. If you like movies, create one that you can walk around in. Write a song and ask a sycamore tree to sing it for you. In the dream world, the only limitation to art is your imagination and your own concepts of what's possible.

Thinking Big

Once you've mastered the basics, you can create things of higher complexity and with more ease. You won't need the security blanket of waking-world logic as you effortlessly manifest and create your surroundings. The following two lucid dreams offer amazing accounts of the potentials of scale, detail, and beauty within creative lucid dreams.

I wanted to create the perfect home. I made a beautiful forest of mostly evergreens and created a clearing for a house. I made a three-story house with many different rooms. Besides the bedrooms, bathrooms, kitchens, dining rooms, and living rooms, I made an enormous library. I also made a planetarium, laboratory, telescope room, and training room. The telescope room possessed different telescopes that could see in every spectrum of electromagnetic radiation. After finishing the house I went outside. I made it night and made the full moon rise into midsky. I made sure there were thunderstorms nearby. I made it so that the wind blew the rain from the nearby storm to the area of our house. The scenario was of astonishing beauty. I then realized that there was one thing missing. She was not present. And I would not create some dream manifestation of her, because it would never be able to measure up to how amazing she is. I could never do such a thing. The dream faded as I woke up.
—RICHARD V. W.

Can't imagine creating a whole house with your mind? In this next example, the dreamer is able to accomplish an even bigger feat.

> This dream, although I have had many other lucid dreams, was the most intense, amazing lucid dream I have ever had. . . . My goal at this point is to create another city, so I fly until I can't see anything I recognize, and sure enough I somehow created another city, this one was at the edge of a body of water and had a beachy feel. I fly down to a waterside marketplace. Around it were weird trees with these odd hanging fruit that sort of glowed, but I went to the marketplace and looked at what type of food my brain had created . . . there were tons of different foods, but the only one I tried was almost like a candy lettuce, it sounds weird, but it was great tasting and very crisp and refreshing. —CAMERON R.

The God Complex

It's important to note that even though these dreamers have a high degree of mastery over the dream world, there are many things not in their control. Richard, despite his detail-oriented approach, was not in control of every color, texture, and intricacy of the home he was building—his subconscious populated those details, filling in the many blanks. He was responsible for the intent (to build a house with specific rooms), but his mind did the rest.

So if you're developing a God complex, put down the thunderbolts and opt for a slice of humble pie.

In dreams, we can create anything, but we're not creating everything. In the second dream, Cameron's intent was to create a city, and he was able to do so. But he did not create each building and street of the city. He simply put his mind to work. The dreamer is surprised to find some candy lettuce that "his brain created." An oneironaut may direct the dream, but the subconscious still does most of the work, slipping in its metaphors and symbols just as it would in any normal dream. Isn't that more fun? Even with complete mastery a lucid dreamer will always be surprised and enlightened by his nighttime adventures. After all, if the ending were predictable, it wouldn't be an adventure.

LUCID DREAMING AS ART

As the world evolves and our level of collective consciousness heightens, the day may come when lucid dreaming itself becomes an art. A place where we craft stories and ideas into visual representation, where we first create our projects and dreams (no pun intended) so that we can more easily bring them into manifestation in the physical world. This is not a new thought. In fact, shamans of indigenous cultures understood that in order for something to be created in the physical world (such as that kitchen you've been meaning to remodel, or this book), it must first be constructed in the "imaginal realm." In other words, lucid dreaming might be a tool in creating our physical reality.

Summary

- The principles of the dream world differ from those of the physical world. You can easily create objects, artwork, or entire landscapes instantly and with vivid accuracy.

- Creation is most effective with a strong intention or image in the mind's eye, an emotional connection, and by "cheating" the law of cause and effect.

- In the dream world, our thoughts and emotions create the world around us instantaneously. Often what we expect to happen will happen.

- We can dream anything into reality. Create your ideal business, craft a poem, write a song, skydive off the Empire State Building, conjure up your soul mate, build your dream home, invent something completely new. Experiencing these things as if they are real will allow you the clarity and confidence to create them in the waking world.

13

The Natives

*The natives . . . are generally tall, straight, well built and of singular
proportion; they tread strong and clever, and mostly walk with a lofty chin.
Their language is lofty, yet narrow . . . and I must say that I know not a
language spoken in Europe, that hath words of more sweetness or greatness,
in accent and emphasis, than theirs.*

—William Penn,
founder of Pennsylvania, pioneer, friend of the Lenape

V enturing through the dream world, we are met with a surprising realization: We are not alone. There are natives in
this land. Some mosey on by, complete strangers wrapped
up in their own world. Others seem to mimic people we know. The
land is different, but the faces are familiar. It appears that all sorts
of intricate dream characters inhabit this world. Some become our
mentors, bestowing upon us advice and offering answers to our most
pressing questions. This world is their turf after all, so they are
natural guides. But not everyone is welcoming. The natives can
scare the crap out of us, appearing in the form of fearsome creatures who hunt us down as we run for our lives.

The natives don't always look like human beings either. Everything is alive and interactive in a dream. You can talk to a flower, ask a teapot a question, or even speak to the dream itself. A friend of ours once had an entire conversation with a bed frame.

Seldom do we stop and think about the characters that populate our dreams, but the question must be asked: Who are these people? It might be easy to write them off as random figments of our imaginations, projections of our own minds that we create subconsciously, but is that all they are? Are dream characters merely background extras, or is there more to them? If you were to speak to them, could they talk back? Might they have something interesting to say?

Now that you're aware inside a dream, it's time to pay attention to the local population. Here you'll discover:

🐝 How dream characters differ from one another.

🐝 Who these natives are.

🐝 How and why you should interact with them.

I decide to spend my time in the dream world more constructively and go look for Chrissie (the woman whom I'd met as a dream guide in the previous lucid dream). I see her across a crowded street, standing in the shadows at the side looking like a spy again . . . I say to her, "What should I do next in life?" She says, "All I can say is it's got something to do with a charity shop and something to do with decoration." And I wake up. —JACK G.

Meet the Natives

As in waking life, you'll meet a variety of characters in the dream world, each character with a different level of awareness. Some are conscious of what's going on around them, some have messages to give, some look like friends or acquaintances, and some are freakin' morons. While you will see a wide range of personalities throughout your explorations, we've found that dream characters (as well as nightmarish figures) gravitate toward one of three basic personality types:

The Sleepwalker
Awareness: low

The Sleepwalker lacks awareness. These characters walk around like Deadheads after a jam-band concert. Try to talk with them and they'll spit out some irrational gibberish. Despite their lack of intelligence, treat the Sleepwalkers as people and not props. What if these characters are important parts of your psyche? Or here's a wild idea: Could they be other dreamers, wrapped up in other dream projections, their own inner worlds invisible to you? Since we're not sure what dream characters are, give them a little respect, will ya?

If your dream was a movie, they'd be the underpaid extras.

The Friend
Awareness: medium-normal
This native doesn't need to be a waking-world buddy of yours to be a friend. These characters are eager to talk and answer questions, and they make excellent conversationalists. They may not understand when you ask them if they know they're dreaming, but they are great allies to have around if you need backup in defeating a nightmare.

If your dream was a movie, they'd be the supporting characters.

The Guide
Awareness: high
This type of native seems to know much more than you do. They usually appear with some important information to communicate, to help guide you through the landscape of the dream world or give you much needed advice about your waking-world problems. These natives will have a quality about them that seems uniquely their own; their presence is quite powerful. Often the dream itself will be stable and sharp when you are around them, as if your own focus and consciousness is somehow affected by theirs. These

natives don't necessarily need to take human form. Guides can come in any shape or size.

If your dream was a movie, they'd be Yoda.

Why You Should Interact with Them

Sure, you can speak and interact with any kind of dream character, but why should you bother? There are many other amazing things to do in a lucid dream after all. We believe this activity is worth your time for the following reasons:

🐝 Guidance. Most notably, dream characters are an excellent reservoir of knowledge and wisdom. Dreamers will benefit greatly by speaking with the natives and asking questions. Go on, ask them something about themselves, about you, or about the dream world. Think of them as your tour guides. They probably have a thing or two to teach you.

🐝 **Healing.** Besides guidance, a run-in with a dream character is an opportunity to heal and learn more about yourself. Say you're dreaming about your friend who passed away many years ago. Speaking to him, asking him questions you may have always wished to ask, could have profound effects on your waking life. Not only that, but facing and confronting aggressive or hostile dream characters can likewise lead to integration and healing.

🐝 **Dream sex.** Here we go. Nearly every lucid dreamer has had dream sex. Even the more spiritual practitioners have gotten down and dirty from time to time. Given the freedom to do whatever you please without limitation, it's completely understandable to follow your natural urges. We won't judge you or try to make you feel guilty, we'd be hypocrites if we did. The lifelike detail of a lucid dream means that dream sex is no exception.

Having sex while lucid can be an incredible experience, but it can also be very distracting. Don't get us wrong, have as much dream sex as you like. Sleep with all the celebrities, rock stars, and crushes you can get your hands on, but just keep an eye on the bigger picture. Remember that you're conscious in the landscape of your own inner world. There is much to explore and discover here, so at some point you'll want to zip up and move on.

Conversing with the Natives

When you come across a dream character, or conjure one to appear, don't waste time on small talk. Who knows how long you have before you wake up or lose lucidity? Use your time wisely. There's no need to dillydally by talking about the weather. Ask the big questions, the ones you really crave the answers to.

Here are some questions you can start with:

- Excuse me, who are you?
- Why are you here?
- Is there something I can help you with?
- Would you like to show me something?
- What is your name?
- Do you represent something important?
- What should I do next in life?
- Where are we?
- Take me on an adventure!
- Can you sing me a song?

GOT A PROBLEM?

Seek out an expert. Dream characters can be very useful guides in helping solve some of our waking-life challenges. Have Albert Einstein explain your dissertation topic to you. Ask Thomas Jefferson to help you understand American politics. Take a walk with your old grandpa or ask a stranger in the dream to help you. You will be pleasantly surprised by the sort of information and insights your dream characters provide.

I notice a young woman not far away, dancing on the beach in a kimono.

Usually I wouldn't care, but something felt odd about her, and I got the sudden urge to investigate. I grab a handful of sand and start walking toward her, slowly letting the sand escape from my hand. . . . She has long dark brown hair, moving about as she dances.

"Hi!"

I don't think she heard me. I have the odd sensation that I somehow know her, but not really. I raise my voice:

"Hello, friend!"

"Oh, hello there!"

I wonder if she's a fellow dreamer, but I'm not really sure how to ask her.

"What are you doing?"

"I'm looking for inspiration for a story I'm writing."

"I see. Dreams are an awesome source of inspiration, aren't they?"

She stops dancing and looks at me surprised.

"You're a dreamer, aren't you?"

"Yes, I am!"

I want to ask her her name, but suddenly she says she's found something, takes off, and flies away. —JEFF Z.

Dream Etiquette

Let's talk about manners. We've been guilty ourselves of this faux pas, but messing around or harassing dream characters is not cool. Some people love to run around in their dreams, treating the natives like playthings. A popular activity among lucid dreamers is to bluntly ask, "Do you know that you don't really exist and you're in my dream?" Almost always, the native will look at you like you're bonkers or they'll get highly offended—I'm not real?!

In a 2005 study at the Harvard Medical School, participants were asked the question "Do your dream characters feel something toward you?" Participants said that 80 percent of the time they sensed that the characters in their dreams felt something. So it's possible that these people have emotions just like anyone else. Do as your mama taught you and treat others the way you want to be treated. If these dream characters are a part of yourself, then that's exactly what you're doing.

What Are Dream Characters?

While you're conversing with the natives, you may start to contemplate the bigger question: "What are dream characters?" You know that they're not just cardboard cutouts, but might they even have the faculties of thought, willpower, and autonomy? Here are two possible answers to that head-scratcher.

🐝 **Projections of you?** No one knows exactly what and who dream characters are. The most logical explanation is that they spring from your subconscious mind; they are you. If the dream world is the realm of your imagination, then the dream characters grow out of your subconscious, as weeds grow from the ground. That's no reason to ignore them of course. If they are a part of your mind, then theoretically they have access to incredible amounts of knowledge and wisdom. Any intelligence and resolve that your dream characters possess come from the well of your subconscious. Ask a dream character something personal, find an answer to an important life question, or simply love them for who they are: YOU.

🐝 **Independent beings?** Bear with us while we get a little "out there." Many lucid dreamers have witnessed the natives displaying curious abilities and behaviors. Frequently some characters act like intelligent, autonomous individuals, many report. Personally, we thought this concept was a bit crazy until we began to have similar experiences. Not all, but some dream characters seemed "otherworldly" and completely conscious. They possessed their own perspective, desires, and motivations and had cognitive abilities. Sometimes these characters were the ones asking the questions and teaching us, and they often seemed sharper than anyone else in the dream world, as if they were in focus while other dream characters were blurry.

Carl Jung ran into the bigger question when he met a wise dream character named Philemon, who returned to him again and again throughout many dreams. The psychotherapist wrote about his experience: "Philemon and other figures of my fantasies brought home to me the crucial insight that there are things in the psyche which I do not produce, but which produce themselves and have their own life. Philemon represented a force that was not myself. In my fantasies I held conversations with him, and he said things which I had not consciously thought."

If this story seems a bit nuts, here's the real puzzler. Many years after Jung dreamed of this figure named Philemon, author Robert Moss dreamed repeatedly of a man who also called himself Philemon. Moss swears that he had never read Jung's writings

> I was kinda obsessed with the idea of dream characters. Because it kinda went to the core of who we are, you know? If I'm conscious and I know I'm in a dream, and this thing is talking to me, and it seems to have its own consciousness, is it separate from me? So I became lucid and I was going through this square—cobblestones—and it was nighttime. I eventually came to this guy and I'm like, "What are you? Are you me or are you you?" He looked at me and rolled his eyes and walked away. So I go up to this other guy and ask, "What are you?" And he just looks at me and says, "That's not important." So, maybe I need to ask a better question. I ask him, "What's important for me to know?" So he looked up at the sky and pondered for a while. "Hmm." Then he looked down and made eye contact with me and said, "You don't do what you want to do." —MATT C.

at the time and was not aware that he shared the same "guide" with the deceased Jung. It was only years later that he made the discovery. And imagine his surprise.

FOOD FOR THOUGHT

Many civilizations believed in some kind of dream sharing, notably the ancient Egyptians, the ancient Chinese, and many indigenous cultures. Do we share more dream experiences than we realize? If this is the case, here are some potential reasons why we are forgetting: (1) We don't remember our dreams, (2) when we dream of someone else, we don't always share it with them the following day, or (3) we are unconsciously consumed by our own private projections while we dream and therefore too wrapped up to connect with our fellow dreamers.

These sorts of experiences make us wonder whether or not there is a shared space, a place that Jung called the collective unconscious. Could it be that dreams act more like the online virtual world Second Life, where we meet other dreamers in a common landscape? Could it be possible to meet our good friends in dreams and share experiences? Are we already doing so and only forgetting? Such a phenomenon, called dream sharing, is already being investigated. It is up to us as conscious dream explorers to find out more and delve into these kinds of experiments.

Coronado's Big Mistake

Francisco Vásquez de Coronado wore his absurdly bulbous metal hat, a sign that he was a Spanish conquistador. But the Indians of the Rio Grande knew very little about Spain. All they knew was that this strange white man was burning down their homes and slaughtering everyone in sight, back in the bitter winter of 1540. That spring, an Indian approached Coronado with tales of a rich, golden city to the north. This man, who the Spaniards called "The Turk," led the conquistadors through the buffalo plains and all the way to central Kansas, a journey that took several months.

They looked everywhere for riches and treasure, but all they found were naked, bow-wielding Indians. "Neither gold nor silver nor any trace of either was found," Coronado famously remarked. The Turk had purposely led Coronado astray so that his people could be free of the conquistadors. He paid for this deception with his life.

You'll have your own encounters with the natives, so let's learn from Coronado's mistake. Be nice to the local population. We don't know who the natives are, and we don't always know exactly what to say to them, but we do know that they are important and deserve our friendship.

Summary

- The natives are not merely cardboard cutouts.

- Each native has his or her own level of awareness; they exist on a spectrum of intelligence and wisdom.

- Dream characters provide guidance, intimacy, and advice, so don't ignore them!

- No one knows exactly what the natives are.

14

Superpowers

What we think, we become.

—Buddha,
spirtual teacher, available in both skinny and tubby varieties

H uman beings have always had the desire for abilities beyond the normal scope of possibility. From the earliest records of human civilization we have been obsessed with gods, the supernatural, and those who exhibit powers of another world. Just look at your local megaplex listings: superhero movie after superhero movie.

Fantasies of the paranormal seep into our imaginations. We ask each other, "If you could have a superpower, what would it be?" knowing full well that this is a thought experiment. But once we pass into the land of dreams, fantasy becomes a reality.

In this chapter we'll open your eyes to skills that you never dreamed were possible. Get ready to leave the constraints of the waking world behind as you discover what you're really capable of.

While you can take on any special power that you desire, for this chapter we've chosen three superhuman talents: shape-shifting, telekinesis, and manipulating energy.

We recommend that you pick a superpower you like and try to stick with it. If you want to give telekinesis a go, don't just attempt it once. While it's fun to try out a superpower, it's even more fun to master it.

Shape-Shifting

Imagine yourself as a dolphin, exploring the sea, or as the president of the United States. What would it feel like to be a cheetah hunting on the African plains? Perhaps you're curious to experience a day as the opposite sex. As your kindergarten teacher told you, you can be anything you want to be, but this time you don't need to wait until you grow up.

Shape-shifting is not new. It's one of the oldest practices of lucid dreamers, especially among the many indigenous cultures of the world. Before we teach you how to shape-shift, it's important to remember that the dream body is completely malleable. The body you inhabit during your dreams is imaginary, a projection of what your mind thinks your body looks like. This projection often changes within our normal dreams. Our friend Matt thought about becoming a woman in his dreams, and suddenly he was a forty-year-old soccer mom. "And the strange thing is that I felt like a woman too," he said.

Shape-shifting is about intentionally altering that self-image, leaving behind the "safety" of your familiar form, transforming into something different.

Keep in mind that shape-shifting requires practice. Our self-image is hardwired into us, a stubborn neural pathway. For most dreamers it will take some time. Don't get frustrated, just keep at it.

1. **Shift your shape**. Before you go to sleep, decide what person, beast, or object that you want to transform into. After a wake-back-to-bed, focus on that intention. If you'd like to become a tiger, imagine what it would be like to have fur or to walk on four muscular limbs. Asleep, you become lucid in your dream, and now it's time to shape-shift. Again, imagine your desired form and make it tactile, feel the sensations that a tiger would feel. Stand on all fours, feel your teeth getting sharp. Close your eyes and say, "When I open my eyes, I will be a tiger." Your dream body can assume whatever shape you want it to.

2. Tigers, oh my! If simply visualizing your form doesn't work, try a shortcut. Because your brain is used to cause and effect, work with your brain rather than against it. Try creating or looking for a potion in the dream world. When your potion is in hand, just say to yourself, "After drinking this potion, I will become a tiger." Gulp! Gulp! Feel free to get creative. How about a magic curtain? Enter a dark cave, get on all fours, and come out as your tiger. You are, in essence, giving yourself a placebo pill, tricking yourself into believing.

3. Mirror image. No luck with the potion? Find a full-length mirror. Then, looking at your reflection, project your shape-shifting thoughts onto the reflection. Watch the reflection's various body parts change. When the reflection has turned into its new form, just step through the mirror.

> I dreamed I was running through the woods, not being chased, just running. I bent down and grabbed the forest floor with my fists and began running with all four limbs. All of a sudden I felt myself changing into some sort of canine. I was amazed at how fast I could run with four legs, how it felt. I was pushing with my back legs and pulling with my front. My center of gravity was completely changed, and I felt what it was like to change into a dog. —MIGUEL H.

4. Sink or swim. Take a leap of faith. Find a body of water, such as a pond, and jump into the water, thinking, "When I hit the water, I'll turn into a giant, golden fish." Or do something really brave: After you've made sure you are in fact dreaming beyond a doubt, jump off a cliff and imagine yourself as a bird, flapping your arms. Confident actions such as these are a sort of bold ultimatum to the dream world. They prove to your subconscious that you are ready and that you believe. Or you can try a shamanic tradition that's a bit more chill. Find a pelt of the animal you want to become and wear it. If your goal is to become a jaguar, for example, wrap your body in a jaguar's hide and feel it becoming yours.

Telekinesis

It's fun to imagine a world where everyone could move objects with their minds. Imagine how easy it would be to clean your room or organize your record collection. The opportunities for practical jokes would be endless. Of course, in the waking world, we lack the ability to do such a thing. This is hardly the case with lucid dreams.

Your ability to move things with your mind will come with focus and confidence. Since telekinesis is about mental power, know that it can happen, and it will.

1. Start small. Once you're lucid, find a small and light object and try to move it a very short distance, so that you can get comfortable and confident in your telekinetic abilities. We take much of the waking world with us into our dreams, such as our understanding of gravity. We've grown to understand that a tennis ball is light, while a car is extremely heavy. Instead of going straight for the cement truck, try lifting a book of matches.

2. Don't stress. There's a chance that your mind won't even make a light object move. Don't get frustrated, you're still becoming accustomed to dream world physics.

Have fun and make it into a noncompetitive game to take the edge off.

3. Extension of the mind. The fabric of your dreams is really just a part of your mind. You use your mind to control your breathing, to move your legs, to focus your thoughts. When you can envision the dream world as a collection of elements, all intertwined with your mind, then you realize that moving a car is just the same as wiggling your pinky. There is no real separation between you and the object. Once you're comfortable with this thought, it's time to move a larger object.

In the dream world, you can feel the connection between you and the "outside world." The entire dream feels alive and conscious, even the air around you pulses with a presence. Remember, you're not manipulating the external forces of gravity: You're manipulating yourself.

The Energy Ball

Controlling and harnessing energy is an incredibly fun skill. Once you can harness energy, you can use it to battle giant robot ninjas, fight monstrous nightmares, and tear down symbolic walls. The idea of harnessing energy can be rather abstract. Most of the time you don't see energy, let alone take command of it. But it's always surrounding you, moving around in the air and through objects. To make this skill less abstract, create an energy ball. An energy ball simply gives you a visual, tangible representation of that energy so that you can control where it goes.

> I parted ways with the ground and soared into the clouds above. One of the bolts of lightning struck me but had no effect. I held out my hand and gathered the lightning into my palm. I proceeded to collect lightning from all around me, all coalescing into a luminous little ball of energy. It sparked and glowed with a soothing blue hue. —RICHARD V. W.

> Focusing on the bike and envisioning what was about to happen, I made a quick arm movement down to the ground, making the bicycle fall over. Furthermore, I noticed a car driving down my street shortly after that and decided I was going to lift it in the air with my mind as it was driving. As it was driving by, I made an upward motion with both of my arms and the car rose about four feet, still in propelled motion, and quickly fell back down again as I let go of my telekinetic hold on it. —BEN S.

1. **Visualize the energy around you.** Trace the electricity that is moving through electric-powered objects in the dream world. See this energy as something visible, such as blue pulsations. If you have trouble doing this, find something that you know has energy. For example look at a light fixture and visualize the energy coming from the wall socket to the lightbulb.

2. **Touch the energy.** Reach out and stick your hand in the energy that is flowing around.

3. **Turn the energy into a ball.** Using your hands as "energy brooms," sweep the energy toward you. As it comes at you, move your hands in a circular motion, as if you're bunching all the energy into a ball. Swirl your hands around the ball to make sure that the energy doesn't get loose.

4. Push the ball away from you. No need to get all intense when making your first energy ball. Simply push the ball away and see what it does. Does it immediately break apart? Does it affect the things it touches? Once this skill becomes second nature, you can start using it however you please.

I think I was in a store, being attacked by evil-satanic witches. I told them they couldn't hurt me because this was a dream, and I have superpowers. They laughed at me.

"Suuure you do," said one of the witches.

"Watch me prove you wrong!" I said. I created a fireball in my hand and threw it at them. I did this repeatedly, and the witches were all jumping around trying to avoid the flaming balls. Next, I shot ice from my hands onto the ground where the witches were standing, and the witches slipped on the ice and collapsed in a heap. This time, I was the one who was laughing. —CELESTE F.

Feel the Power

Superpowers can be a lot of fun, but they do serve a purpose. Spend an hour shooting energy balls into the night sky and you'll probably wake up feeling powerful and confident. After you're able to move cars with your mind, what insignificant day-to-day problems can stand in your way? If you're capable of doing the impossible in a dream, don't forget that the waking world is a place of possibility too. Be sure to take that feeling of confidence and empowerment with you. Remember that under your modest work clothes hide a pair of tights and a cape.

WHITE MAGIC

Energy can be used to create as well as destroy. It can be used to fight off monsters, but it can also help power your lucid dream creations. Say you're building a rocket ship that just won't take off. Direct all the surrounding energy toward the rocket ship and give it the push it needs. And what about healing yourself? By manipulating the energy around you, you're becoming aware of the fabric of the dream.

> I remembered to do a reality check and realized I was dreaming. I set out to do my lucid task, transforming into a bird and flying. I leaped up into the air and threw my arms wide. My arms turned into huge wings and the rest of my body followed. My feathers were bright red, with orange tips on some of them. When the transformation was complete, I flapped my wings as hard as I could and took off flying. I was going really slow, as if swimming through water. I tried moving my wings slower and with more control, and it worked. I was flying much faster. —ANTHONY P.

Summary

- Superpowers are totally possible inside dreams.

- The limits of your abilities directly relate to your focus and confidence.

- Your dreams can be a place without gravity, where the definition of "you" is unstable and where your mind can control objects and energy at will.

- Take your sense of confidence and power into the waking world.

PART FIVE

MASTERING

the

TERRAIN

Y ou know the land. You know the people. You've worked hard and it's paying off. Very likely the landscape has already revealed some amazing wonders. The dream world is no longer the foggy memory of a foreign world but a destination you visit with complete clarity every night. The barrier between possible and impossible is rapidly blurring. Your adventure has only just begun.

You may not be there yet. Perhaps you're still working on remembering your dreams, or giving a go at the wake-back-to-bed technique (page 101). Not to worry, you'll have plenty of time to practice, a few hours every night in fact.

The dream world is vast. In the upcoming chapters, as we leave the lush grass and rolling hills, your surroundings transition to a sparser, rocky place. The road ahead is more challenging to navigate, the map is harder to read, but the rewards are greater than before.

Here, you will come face-to-face with aspects of yourself. It's time to tackle those hopes and fears that have been waiting patiently (or not so patiently) on the cusp of your subconscious. Like Odysseus, you will battle monsters, overcome challenges, and learn to heal yourself. And all before breakfast.

15

Defusing Nightmares

Fear has its use but cowardice has none.

—Mahatma Gandhi,
nonviolent activist, lawyer, walking enthusiast

E vil gremlins, masked psychopaths, satanic witches, mutated zombie brains, little girls climbing out of wells. We'll happily pay good money for one of these popcorn flicks, to feel like we're getting chased by a chain saw–wielding maniac or some other monster. We love to get the crap scared out of us. But when these dark figures show up in our dreams, it gets a little too real.

Nightmares are the dark underbelly of the dream world, bringing out intense feelings of fear, terror, distress, or anxiety. And they don't just happen when we're young; about 5 to 10 percent of adults have at least one or more nightmares a month. In a study of 439 German students, an average of about two nightmares per month were reported, a statistic backed up by a separate study of

Chinese students. Whether you're being chased, attacked, intimidated, or find yourself suddenly naked in public, nightmares are always emotionally charged. Even after you wake, your heart is still racing and your stomach is twisted in a tight knot. You may tell yourself "it was just a dream," but the physical and emotional toll it takes on you is very real.

Dreams serve as internal status reports. They reflect how we are feeling in our waking life. So it makes sense that stress, illness,

The town is happy. The people are happy. The sun is out and everything is good in the world. All of a sudden about a half dozen *Mad Max/Devil's Reject*-esque thugs come cruising into town. They start trouble and then knock me out. I awaken in a dark and dirty jail cell with the door open. As I leave the jail, I notice that the town is no longer happy. It is full of darkness, misery, and pain. It is hell on earth. As I start exploring this nightmare, I begin to stumble across the "happy" people from earlier. But they are no longer happy, because they are dead. When I approach their dead bodies, I'm instantly sent back to relive the last minute of their life. It always starts with them hiding or running from one of the bad guys. Despite where I/they run to, they always get caught and are brutally murdered. Right before they die, I'm sent back into my own body. This happens over and over again. I end up finding at least seven bodies, where I relive their deaths. The dream ends when the bad guys find me in my body and chase me down. I'm about to be killed and then I wake up. —JARED Z.

troubled relationships, or traumatic events can manifest themselves as dark forces come nighttime. If we have been avoiding something in our daily lives, it will soon find a means to get our attention. Nightmares might also be our subconscious's response to physical conditions such as illness, fever, medication, the use of certain drugs (or a rapid withdrawal of them), upcoming life changes, pregnancy, financial concerns, or a change in jobs.

Fortunately it's possible to completely vanquish a nightmare in a lucid dream. Like a bomb squad disarming a land mine, in this chapter we'll teach you how to defuse your nightmares. We'll also bring you in on a little secret: how to use nightmares as a shortcut to becoming lucid. Nocturnal demons can be so frightening that some people consciously commit to forgetting and repressing all of their dreams, ignoring these urgent messages. If you are such a person, don't you worry. This chapter will give you the simple tools you need.

Integration of Our Shadow Elements

Although it might not seem like it, our nightmares are not trying to scare us—they are trying to get across an important message. Carl Jung refers to nightmares as "shadow elements." He believed that they are missing parts of ourselves. Nightmares seem to reflect undesirable aspects of our psyches that we have unconsciously rejected, disowned, or denied. Like neglected puppies, they just want to be loved and embraced, accepted back into our lives. In Jung's eyes, if we accept our nightmares and integrate them into our psyches, we'll be on the way toward becoming whole and balanced people.

In waking life, we try to overcome our fears. If you were to overcome a fear of heights, for example, the resolution of your phobia would open up more possibilities and a fuller, richer life. Finally you can take that trip to the Grand Canyon. Resolving nightmares works in the same way. By solving the problems of the dream and facing what's plaguing you, the result is more freedom, less internal conflict, and a more balanced perspective.

The longer your nightmares stay hidden in your subconscious, the more damage they'll do. You can deal with nightmares during the day by talking about them with your friends and family or by writing them down in your journal. Acknowledging them in your daily life is the first step in treating them, letting the sun fill in the darker shadows. You can also vanquish them at night while lucid. Our dreams might not be the first place our demons show up, but luckily they can be the last.

Using Lucidity to Face a Nightmare

In a nightmare, we lack a sense of control. Lucid dreaming is an empowering tool to face nightmares and heal through them. In fact, for the oneironaut, nightmares are a perfect springboard to trigger lucidity. Running away from something or being scared for your life—these situations can actually serve as dream signs. Therefore, next time you find yourself in a hot pursuit or mortally afraid, ask yourself if you're dreaming.

Stephen LaBerge tells us of one such event in his book *Exploring the World of Lucid Dreaming*. He was on the phone with his seven-year-old niece when she told him of a horrible dream: She was swimming in a local reservoir when a shark attacked her. LaBerge, being the maverick lucid dreamer that he is, told his niece that the next time she sees a shark, she'll know that she's inside a dream. Since nothing bad can happen in dreams, she could make friends with the shark. A week later his niece called back: "Do you know what I did? I rode on the back of that shark."

Sometimes nightmares are standard hero-in-danger narratives.

> I am being chased by the guy from the *Halloween* movies, the guy with the white mask, Michael Myers. I'm aware of his presence in the house. He just seems to keep killing people. It is nighttime, and I think, "As long as we can make it to the daytime, we'll be all right." But then the daytime comes and he is still chasing us. He doesn't run fast, he is just always there. We shoot him, and we think he is dead . . . but no, he is not. There is a final standoff on this steel bridge. The last thing I remember is running right at him. —DEREK A.

Other times there is no actual antagonist, but just a pervasive feeling of anxiety or dread. We've all had the dream where we're late to a class (there's an essay due tomorrow?) or a tooth falls out (it will never grow back!) or we're naked in public. It's not the subject matter that turns a dream into a nightmare; it's the feeling you get while trapped inside the dream.

No matter what kind of nightmare it is, the only way to get rid of it completely is to face it head-on.

I'm walking down a white hallway in some very plain building. Up ahead there are two guys walking toward me. I turn to my right to open the door closest to me. It's locked. The two men are now walking fast toward me. I turn around and start running. The hallway becomes longer to the point where it's nearly two football fields long. As I'm running, I can hear them behind me getting closer. The thought crosses my mind, "What am I doing?" I continue to run as a dialogue plays in my head. "Am I dreaming? Yes! Of course I'm dreaming!" I decide to stop running and face these attackers. Immediately when I turn around they too stop running, and begin walking over to me. I still feel fear in approaching these men. What do they want? I remind myself that I'm in a dream and find acceptance and love in myself. I try to project this compassion toward my pursuers. Immediately, I feel safe and protected. Nothing can harm me. One of the men holds his hand out, as if wanting to shake my hand. His hand is on fire. He tells me, "Don't let your flame go out." I shake his hand. It feels warm and powerful. I thank him, and the dream ends. I wake up feeling empowered. —THOMAS P.

Once challenged, your hostile dream figure or feeling will usually lose its power and diminish in size, becoming as harmless as a kitten. According to the Senoi people of Malaysia, when we confront a nightmare, we conquer it. Now that it's defused, as a lucid dreamer you can question the once shadowy figure. Normally, dreams speak to us in the language of symbols and metaphors. But if you bluntly ask the nightmare what its purpose is, often it will clearly state with words what it was trying to tell you with metaphors. Chat away with your demons and discover their hidden messages.

Going Toe-to-Toe with a Nightmare:
TIPS FOR FACING YOUR FEARS

In the red corner, weighing in at well over two thousand pounds, the heavyweight champion of nightmares, the beast from the East, the skeleton in your closet, repressed and back for revenge, Mister . . . Demon Bear!

And in the blue corner, the mind behind it all, the creator of the dream itself, lucid and ready to tackle, the Dream Explorer!

Ding ding! Here are some tips on how to deliver the KO punch:

1. Wherever You Go, There You Are
In horror movies, the damsel who runs upstairs never makes it out alive. Don't get clever and think that you can run away from your nightmares. Many people think that they can outsmart their nightmares by flying away or switching dream scenes. Remember this

saying: Wherever you go, there you are. Even if you fly across the ocean to another planet or change the dream completely, your nightmare will often manifest itself wherever you are. Recurring nightmares happen when we continually run from the same fear. If it has an important message, your subconscious is not going to quit until it has delivered it.

2. Pulling the Cord

Many people feel relieved when they wake themselves up just before a nightmare gets too close, which is always an option. Imagine you've got a parachute strapped to your back. You can yank on the cord at any time and a tether will pull you back to the waking world, safe and sound. Phew, bullet dodged! So when you encounter a nightmare, why not just wake yourself up every time? Imagine that your kitchen stove caught fire and burst into flames. Would you move into the living room, flip the TV on, and pretend nothing is wrong? Sooner or later your stove will burn down the entire house. Continuously escaping from parts of yourself that demand to be heard can be harmful to both your dream life and your waking life. When we repress these messages, we repress our self-awareness. We're left with an unresolved conflict, like a cough that won't go away. With that said, if things get too intense and you need to get out to collect yourself, remember you can always pull the cord.

3. Know You Are Safe

That bothersome beast, person, or object cannot actually hurt you. In fact, you'll be doing more harm to yourself by running away from it. If your nightmare is acting like a bully and physically threatening you, it's all talk. Just like a dog biting its own tail, what you're really battling is a part of yourself. Love thy nightmare.

4. Don't Change the Dream, Change Yourself

When lucid, the goal isn't to control the situation or the nightmare. Attempting to quarantine or kill it will just make it angry. Aggression, according to lucid dreamer Paul Tholey, will often make the nightmarish figure stronger. And it makes sense: You're playing right into its power by thinking that it *has* power. Focus on your own emotions and release positive and loving feelings toward your nightmare. This might sound very difficult, but under the guise of lucid dreaming, and with total awareness, calmly focus on changing yourself, not the dream. What emotions are you feeling? Let go of anxiety and fear and watch as that gruesome demon bear transforms into a cute teddy.

5. Enlist Some Reinforcements

If you don't want to face your fears alone, we don't blame you. Lucky for you, there are plenty of people on your side in the dream world. Call upon an ally or a guide to help you tag-team your (peaceful) confrontation. Perhaps you want King Arthur to watch your back, or enlist Gandhi to talk things out? You can conjure a guide with a strong intention or incubation (see Chapter 17). Or instead of finding a dream character to help, you can use your own superpowers to build up confidence for your confrontation. Imagine a force field of protection around you, increase the size of your dream body, whatever gives you the feeling of power and safety that you need. Go get 'em!

WRITING THE NEXT CHAPTER

Ever had a recurring nightmare? This exercise involves imagining yourself finishing that persistent dream with a different ending. Eventually this practice will filter into your dreams, and the next time you have a nightmare you'll become lucid without even trying.

While awake, think back to a nightmare you had and imagine yourself back in the present moment of that dream. Sit quietly and replay the nightmare in your mind once or twice in the way it actually occurred.

Now, replay it a third time, but this time picture yourself becoming aware that you're dreaming. Imagine the realization suddenly dawning on you in the middle of your nightmare. I'm dreaming. Picture yourself calmly facing the source of your fear, asking what it represents. Project love and acceptance to the dark figure in front of you. It is you, so why wouldn't you love it?

Dialogue with the Nightmare

Sometimes defusing a nightmare requires no dialogue at all. Simply face your foe head-on—that could be all the treatment you need. But be curious! Here's your chance to reveal some really interesting stuff about yourself. Ask your nightmarish demon questions like:

- Why are you chasing me?
- What do you want?
- Who are you?
- Why am I in this situation?
- How can I help you?
- What do you represent?
- What do you have to teach me?

TELL IT TO THE SUN!

The Greeks believed that some dreams foretold the future. After a bad dream, they would purify themselves by bathing in cold water, telling their dream to the sun, and even performing sacrifices to protective deities.

The dark figure prowls behind you, tense and brooding. It's been on your tail for weeks. It pounces forward—a throaty howl—then retreats back into the shadows, watching and waiting. When we are plagued by inner turmoil, we feel weakened, blocked, and outright crappy. Our minds get stuck in a continual funk of imbalance. Even though it's "just a dream," a nightmare can affect your entire life. Your relationships, your career, and your own emotional and physical health become threatened. Use nightmares as a signpost that something needs your care and attention. This journey isn't just fun and games. Facing your nightmare might be a challenge, but this leg of the adventure will lead toward a happier and more integrated you.

Summary

- Use your nightmares as triggers for lucidity and get to the bottom of what is plaguing you.

- The ultimate goal of the ghastly figure is not to hurt you; it wants to communicate a message and to gain your acceptance. Like a little kid acting out, it just wants to be heard.

- Ask your nightmare questions and bring to light the repressed demons of your subconscious.

- Wave your white flag and surrender to the conflict—you will become paradoxically strong. Instead of aggression, face your pursuer with love and humility.

- The effects of healing a nightmare while it's taking place will carry over into your waking life and enrich you with new energy.

16

Healing and Wholeness

The power which a man's imagination has over his body to heal it or make it sick is a force which none of us is born without. The first man had it; and the last one will possess it.

—Mark Twain,
author, humorist, didn't let school ruin his education

In the fourth century BCE, in the jagged and mountainous coast of southern Greece, you arrive at one of the first hospitals of the ancient world. Dedicated to Aesculapius, the Greek healer and son of Apollo, this temple attracts droves of the crippled and sick who've made pilgrimages in the hope of a cure for their ailments. Entering one these temples, you are not searching for medicine, you are looking for a dream. Your stomach rumbles—you've fasted for days in preparation. You lie down on the hard stone and fall asleep. You hope that the gods will appear in your dreams and show you a cure. Inscribed on the temple walls are the stories of previous visitors, whose ailments, including chronic illnesses such as blindness, were reported to have vanished with the help of dreams.

Fast-forward a few millennia. There's no such thing as a dream temple anymore, but our bodies and minds haven't changed all that much.

As science is finding out, your body can't even differentiate between a thought and a real-life event. Images of delicious hamburgers can make you salivate, a homework assignment can make you anxious, a funny movie can make your whole body shake with laughter, and a beautiful member of the desired sex can cause . . . other physical reactions. "The mind lives in every cell of the body," writes neuroscientist Candace Pert. The power the mind has over the body can have revolutionary effects.

If movies and hamburgers can twist our bodies into knots, then what about lucid dreams? In a lucid dream, you're the writer and the director; the scenes are created by your imagination and feel very realistic. Compared to a mere thought, a lucid dream is real in every sense of the word. Even though your physical body lies in your bed, it is still influenced by the intense emotions and perceptions of your dreaming mind. It seems that the ancient Greeks got it right: We can actually heal through the experiences of a dream.

People are often skeptical when we suggest that they can heal through a lucid dream. But evidence for this phenomenon comes from hundreds of firsthand accounts from today's dreamers, and the practice spans back not only to Greeks but also to the ancient Egyptians and dozens of other cultures throughout the world.

Using lucid dreams to heal is a very practical, commonsense practice. Cut off from all outside world distractions, the dreamer has the opportunity to communicate directly with his or her subconscious and heal through it. Modern medicine tries to heal us from the outside in, while dream healing mends from the inside out. As with hypnosis, the power of your subconscious is being tapped. In this chapter, we'll separate dream healing into two categories: mental and physical.

Healing the Mind

According to psychologist Abraham Maslow, the main goal of all therapy is integration. Integration means coming together or fusing. In psychological terms, it's the process whereby the psyche becomes whole. Even if we don't need to see a psychologist, many of us do not live to our fullest potential simply because we lack unity within. We are held back by the nagging voices of our fears, doubts, and criticisms. A block forms, preventing us from expressing who we really are and from living a rewarding life.

Many mental problems seem to happen when we're repressing parts of ourselves. If a traumatic event occurred when we were young, we may lock that experience away in order to cope. Psychologists call this *dissociation*. Shamans throughout the world have called it soul loss.

A healthy person is a united, integrated person whose memory, emotions, social functions, body, etc., are all connected as a united system.

We become unhealthy when one or more of these aspects become disconnected from the system, and we become detached, numb, anxious, or depressed. You can go to a therapist for help in these matters, nothing wrong with that. But in addition to therapy, lucid dreaming can be a powerful tool.

Becoming Whole in Dreams

In Old English, the word *healing* means "to make whole." Dreams often alert us to our problems and guide us toward integration. Think of dreams as an intuitive, concerned mother, putting the back of her hand to your forehead to see if you're okay.

Read over your dream journal entries and ask yourself,

> After a hard breakup, for months I didn't feel like myself. I was depressed, confused, and bitter over the way things had ended. Knowing I could ask the dream to heal me, I set out to incubate a dream in which it would heal me of my suffering. A couple of days later, I had the most vivid lucid dream. I was with my ex-girlfriend at the time and we were sitting on a park bench. She took my hand and with a gentle voice said, "I guess it's time I forgive you, huh?" I nodded as I looked into her eyes. "I think so." I woke up feeling incredible. I had the closure I needed to move on. From that day on, I have felt nothing but warmth and acceptance toward the entire situation. —MARTY M.

I found myself talking with a man in a room. Not sure what we were talking about but something out on the balcony caught my attention. I walked out onto the balcony and instantly an orb, or what I took to be an actual sun, whizzed by above my head. A second sun followed, and the two danced in the sky. I watched as the clouds began changing above me. These weren't earthly clouds, these were cosmic clouds and I could see within them millions of stars. The sky changed again, this time revealing an enormous whale made of light. The whale swam through the cosmos like water. Then I saw the most beautiful light in the world. It was the purest white but at the same time it gave off the most incredible hues of greens, blues, and pinks. I watched the sky in complete awe, humbled at the magnitude of what I was seeing. It was incredible, and it brought me to tears. The man hugged me from behind and let me cry. I felt like I was healing. The dream changed and I asked where we were and someone said, "San Pablo." I then heard a voice that told me something very profound: "All matter has its origin in Spirit," it said. I woke up with a renewed sense of energy and excitement. —THOMAS P.

"Do any of these dreams contain advice on how I can be happier and more whole?" We can record and interpret our normal dreams in order to decode the messages from our subconscious. Sometimes, however, interpreting our dream journals can be tough. It's not always possible to know exactly what your subconscious is communicating. This is where lucid dreaming comes in. You can find lost parts of yourself while actively exploring your inner world.

🐝 **Olly olly oxen free!** Use your intuition and look for dream characters who may be symbols of your emotional difficulties or repressed experiences. They may come in the form of sad or injured people, children (your lost inner child?), or a less obvious symbol created by your imagination.

🐝 **Let's get together.** You find a person or thing that may be a hidden aspect of yourself. Great! Try reuniting with it somehow. It may be as easy as a passionate intention: "I want to become whole." For example, maybe your problem is lack of energy.

If you come across a dream character who's bursting with energy, maybe you've found your lost energetic self. Try drawing out its energy and absorbing it through the pores of your skin.

🐝 **Create experiences.** Create a visual to heal yourself. If you're anxious, use dream incubation or a transportation technique and journey to a pristine jungle waterfall. Before you bathe in the water, tell yourself that the water heals anxiety. Find an ex-boyfriend (your projection of him) and find closure to your relationship. Think of the images and experiences that may jolt you out of your emotional funk.

🐝 **Use caution.** If you've gone through traumatic events in the past, and addressing these problems alone is too much to handle, seek out a therapist or professional. You can still use the tool of lucid dreaming in conjunction with therapy. Don't be shy, tell your doc about lucid dreaming and what you plan to do.

Physical Healing and the Power of Images

If our minds are powerful enough to make ourselves sick, we're powerful enough to make ourselves well. Healing the body through a lucid dream may sound like magic, but if we see the body and mind as one connected entity, then of course the mind can influence the body, and vice versa. Let's pause here before you get the wrong idea. Lucid dreaming is not a replacement for Western medicine, but it can be used in conjunction with physical treatments or procedures. In fact, many cancer centers offer guided imagery in conjunction with chemotherapy. Guided imagery is similar to dream healing. Patients are led through waking-world exercises in which they daydream intricate images, such as Pac-Man wandering through the body and eating all the cancer cells. These images are self-designed to promote health. The American Cancer Society notes that "a review of forty-six studies that were conducted from 1966 to 1998 suggested that guided imagery may be helpful in managing stress, anxiety, and depression and in lowering blood pressure, reducing pain, and reducing some side effects of chemotherapy." In addition to cancer treatment, guided imagery has been proven to help patients with allergies, diabetes, heart disease, and carpal tunnel syndrome.

Daytime imagery is great, but who's to say that lucid dreaming might not have an even bigger impact? As we've learned, the mind does not distinguish between a thought and a real-life event. And a dream is not just a thought or an image; it's a tapestry woven from all five senses—a full-fledged experience.

An Image Is Worth a Thousand Words

The old cliché describes it perfectly. All you need to help heal yourself in a lucid dream are a few specific images that you can use to affect the body through the mind. In the end it's up to you to create the images and experiences that are personal to you, that will help you heal. There are, however, some common visualizations and techniques. While it's effective to daydream these experiences, we suggest trying them in a lucid dream.

The Colored Light

Light is a common archetype that dreamers experience when healing themselves. Try feeling your specific intent to heal, really feel it. Then imagine a healing glow emanating from your hands or finger (think of E.T. phoning home). Most dreamers find that the image of this light is all they need to heal, a powerful punch from their subconscious.

The Voodoo Doll

Try imagining your illness or obstacle as an object or group of objects. You can either think up this metaphor yourself or ask the dream to do it for you. For example, if your goal is to eradicate a pain in your thigh, perhaps you want to dream of the pain as a small fire burning down a pile of dry leaves. Find a nearby bucket of water, douse the fire, and imagine extinguishing your waking body's pain at the same time.

The Healer

In your lucid dream, try seeking out an animal or human to do the healing for you. This can be done with intention or by calling out to the dream itself, "Bring me to someone who can help heal me." Most likely, someone will appear. This entity is a strong symbol: Your subconscious has summoned it and given it the strength and authority to heal you.

I had been stressed because of school and I was physically sick with the flu. I fell asleep and became lucid. A man approached me. He had these bright blue eyes. He looked at me and said, "You're sick." I suddenly felt very good. The feeling traveled through my body. It was like nothing I have experienced. I was healed by him. He grabbed my shoulders, and his eyes were becoming even more blue . . . I was healed, I know that. I'm not sure if it was me healing myself or maybe it was a guide helping me. —GEORGE G.

The Balancing Act

Your health is much more than just your physical well-being. Your emotions, beliefs, and underlying view of the world come into play. Your physical symptoms are often a result of an emotional or spiritual imbalance. As our good friend Carl Jung notes, "not infrequently the dreams show that there is a remarkable inner symbolic connection between an undoubted physical illness and a definite psychic problem." With dreaming, you can tap into your subconscious's power to heal. But don't ignore your doctor's orders. In conjunction with physical treatments, dream healing can alleviate physical ailments and can bring balance to your emotional, spiritual, and mental well-being.

Summary

Images have a powerful influence over the mind and body.

- You can create specific, creative, visual experiences with lucid dreaming in order to heal yourself.

- It seems to be possible to improve physical health with a dream.

- Use dreams to become mentally whole by reuniting with lost parts of yourself.

17

Dream Incubation

Every one of us has in him
a continent of undiscovered character.
Blessed is he who acts the Columbus to his own soul.

—Theodore Ledyard Cuyler,
religious writer, liked flowers more than statues

A
nna Kingsford was one of the very first English women
to boast a medical degree. A vegetarian, she was the only
student of her time to obtain a medical degree without
experimenting on animals. It was the late nineteenth century,
and as a strong-willed feminist, animal activist, and student of
Buddhism, life was an uphill battle for Kingsford. One morning,
in 1877, she recorded this dream:

> *Having fallen asleep last night while in a state of great*
> *perplexity about the care and education of my daughter,*
> *I dreamt as follows. I was walking with the child along the*

border of a high cliff, at the foot of which was the sea.
The path was exceedingly narrow, and on the inner side
was flanked by a line of rocks and stones. A voice of
someone close at hand suddenly addressed me; and on
turning my head I found standing before me a man in
the garb of a fisherman. . . . He stretched out his hand to
take the child, saying he had come to fetch her, for that
in the path I was following there was room only for one.
"Let her come to us," he added; "she will do very well
as a fisherman's daughter."
—Anna Kingsford, November 3, 1877

Sleep on it.

That's the advice we often get when pondering over a big life
change. Of course, what is meant by the phrase is more along the
lines of "give it some time." However, once you've mastered the
simple art of dream incubation, "sleeping on it" will mean something totally new.

Nowadays our society tends to see dreaming as something that
is happening to us. Dreams are inflicted upon us like a case of
the measles. We lie down, conk out, and maybe remember some
fragments in the morning. You've started to learn how to wake
up in your dreams, but what if you could decide what dream you
were going to have before you dreamed it? As you prepare for bed,
you can decide upon a dream location, a theme, or even a person
you want to meet. Instead of letting your subconscious call all the
shots, you can have some say in the matter, incubating a dream just
like a hen incubates her egg.

Ask to have a dream about that friend you haven't seen in years. Incubate an exciting boat ride to the Indian Ocean. Want to be the queen of England for an hour? The choice is yours.

You don't have to be lucid to perform dream incubation. Lucid dreaming is about influencing the dream once you're in it; dream incubation allows you to set the stage for your dream before bed. After we explain the easy practice of dream incubation, we'll talk about how you can combine dream incubation with lucid dreaming, a killer hybrid of two powerful techniques.

Rub a Dying Guinea Pig on Your Body

Dream incubation is not new: Ancient Egyptians incubated dreams way back when. If they had an important question or problem, they'd travel to a dream temple where they'd be closer to a particular god. The Egyptian subjects would pose their question to the gods before falling asleep in the temple. Then they'd dream, in hopes of receiving divine advice about their troubles.

Dream incubation techniques were developed in other parts of the world as well, and they often got

> I asked my dreams what maturity or adulthood means to me. Strength, knowledge, responsibility? I dream of a round pool in a Roman atrium, cupped in a columned arcade, half sun, half shade. It's the home of a mermaid who usually doesn't let visitors get too close. But to my surprise, she invites me in to swim. She tells me, "I won't die till love dies." "I . . . I'm not sure what you mean." She smiles and says, "I'll live as long as human beings who can love still live." —CHRIS W.

pretty weird. The Quechua Indians of Peru would perform a sleep incubation ritual that would start with the patient being rubbed from head to toe with a live guinea pig. It was done in such a way that the guinea pig would die by the end of the procedure. Afterward the animal would be skinned and from the blood and entrails a diagnosis would be read. Other methods include predream fasting, sleeping in trees, or even inserting splints and ropes under the subject's skin.

Don't worry, we won't ask you to go on a fast or rub dying guinea pigs on your body. In fact, when you strip away all the theatricals, dream incubation is really simple. All you're doing is prepping your mind for a particular dream to happen. That's it.

In these cultures, theatrics served a simple role: They made the dreamer believe that their wish would be granted. The rituals were effective because they gave weight and importance to the idea of dream incubation. But if you trust in the process of dreaming, you don't need weird rituals. All you need is a solid intention.

Want to dream you're on the moon? Before you go to bed, ask to have a dream of being on the moon. Want to know if you should switch careers? Incubate a dream that will help you figure it out.

A 1993 study shows the effectiveness of dream incubation. At Harvard Medical School, seventy-six students were taught how to incubate. For one week, the subjects went to sleep trying to incubate a dream that would solve a particular problem. One half of the students reported a dream that related to their problems. "Seventy percent of these believed their dream contained a solution to the problem," the study concludes. The student's dream journals were rated by judges, and the reports were confirmed.

How to Incubate a Dream

1. **Scribble down your intention.** Want to go fly-fishing on Mars? Write it down. Want to party with a polar bear? The more specific the intention is, the better. A specific intention sends a clear signal to your subconscious. You can even ask questions that you want to be answered in your dream, such as "What should I study in college?" If you do ask a question, be careful to steer clear of yes or no questions, they tend to produce very vague answers.

The more vivid and visceral the intention is, the more effective it will be: "I want to dip my toes in the Mediterranean sea" is a far more effective intention than "I want to go to the beach." Often, just thinking about your intention a few times before bed does the trick. You may not get exactly the dream that you asked for, but it will be something close.

Here are a few examples of dreams you could incubate, but when it comes down to it, your imagination is the limit:

- I will dream that I am flying in a small, red plane during sunset.
- I will dream that I have become a focused, diligent student.
- I will dream that I see a new idea for a sculpture, already created.
- I will dream that I'm walking around my old childhood home in the summer.
- I will dream that my grandma will give advice on my marriage.
- I will dream that I am having a conversation with my future self, twenty years older.

2. Bravo, Picasso. Draw a picture to accompany the written intention. Draw a specific image and try to keep it simple and clear. Try drawing and writing down your intention in your dream journal, on the left side of the page. Then, when you wake up in the morning, record your dreams as usual on the right side. As you read over your dreams, it will be easy to see if your intentions (left) match up with the results (right). You'll be surprised how often your incubated dreams hatch.

3. Put the intention under your pillow. Might sound a bit superstitious, like you're waiting for the Dream Fairy to come and drop you a nickel. But remember that dreaming is all about the mind, and if you can send yet another message to your brain that you want to incubate a dream, why not try it? Put your textual or visual intention under your pillow. Maybe the Dream Fairy will stop by after all.

4. Make up your own ritual. Everyone has their own rituals: waking up, taking a shower, getting into a car, etc. Before you incubate a dream, figure out a routine that makes the process focused, fun, and important. Take a bath before sleep, listen to a special song— whatever. Anything except lighting a candle. (Unless, that is, you want to incubate a small fire in your bedroom.) Like the ancient Egyptians, create a sacred space, whatever that means for you, and focus your mind on your desired dream.

Keeping the Egg Warm

Just as an egg needs lots of warmth from its mommy before it hatches, you need to give your dream some lovin'. The heat comes in the form of passion. Remember that the key principle of a good intention is "juice." The more passion you feel toward your desire, the more effective the incubation process will be.

Your subconscious can tell if your heart's not in it.

If you ask casually for a dream about, say, a "fun day in the park," your subconscious will treat your intention with the same passivity. But if you pump that intention full of life, with burning desire and urgency, your subconscious will respond with the same energy.

Typically, the dreams that incubate the best are related to wishes for healing, resolving deep loss, or other highly emotional, burning intentions. If your intention isn't already charged with emotion, do what great actors do and find a way to connect your intention to a deep emotion within you.

For example, if your intention is to fly through the clouds, think about how freeing that experience would be. Maybe the sensation of flying will help you with a debilitating anxiety problem that you have during waking life. You want to cure this problem badly, so your subconscious will oblige, giving you a dream about flying. If your intention is to walk through your childhood home, conjure up all those heavy feelings of nostalgia, pain, or love that are connected to the house.

Hatching the Egg

As you fall asleep, repeat the intention in your head, remembering to think of one specific sentence. For optimal results, perform a wake-back-to-bed technique before you incubate a dream. Instead of trying to become lucid, you'll focus on that one image that sums up your intention. Imagine all the sensations and memories that are attached to it. Let your mind bathe in it.

Upon waking, recall and record the dream with as much detail as possible. It may contain important information, guidance, or good feelings that you can slip into your pocket and use during waking life.

It had been nearly ten years since my stepmom's father had passed. I was speaking to her one evening about dreaming, particularly lucid dreaming. I said to her, "If this were a dream right now, what would you want to do?" "I'd want to see my dad," she said. "I'd want to hear his voice again." I told her that this was possible, and that tonight she could make that happen through dream incubation. She went to bed that night with a burning desire repeating over and over: her intention to see her dad in her dreams. I woke up the next morning to see her in the kitchen. She had tears in her eyes. "I saw him! I saw my dad. It was so real. He was there with me in the living room. I talked with him and I gave him a hug. I could feel him. I can't believe it." —THOMAS P.

Thomas's stepmom experienced the power that dreams have for healing. For the first time in ten years, she was able to hug her dad. All she had to do was ask her subconscious for that dream, it was that simple. Something she never knew was possible became very real. That memory will be with her for the rest of her life.

Incubating Lucid Dreams

As with all other aspects of dreaming, being conscious during a dream opens up new possibilities. Let's raise the stakes a bit by throwing the word *lucid* into the dream incubation process. First off, you can use dream incubation as a method to become lucid.

Beyond that, if you become lucid while inside your incubated dream, that dream will be more useful and powerful.

Incubation as a Trigger

Stephen LaBerge and Howard Rheingold, in their book *Exploring the World of Lucid Dreaming,* note that you can use dream incubation as a trigger. Let's say you incubate a dream about flying in an airplane. You spend an hour before bed visualizing the interior of the plane, the wind against your cheeks, and the clouds flying by. Before you know it, you are in an airplane, feeling all these things. "Wait a minute," you think, "isn't this the very dream I was trying to incubate? I must be in that dream now!" Because you are aware and conscious, the experience will be heightened.

Setting the Stage

While many lucid dreams have the aimlessness of playing in a sandbox, an incubated lucid dream allows you to go after specific goals. For example, instead of wasting precious time looking for your deceased grandmother, you can begin the dream sitting in her living room, staring at her smiling face. Solve a specific problem, talk to a specific person, and look for the exact guidance that you seek. You've asked your subconscious to set the stage for your lucid dream, and now you can act out your role in the play.

Flap Your Wings

Remember the picture book *Flap Your Wings* by P. D. Eastman? Allow us to jog your memory. One day an egg falls into the nest of Mr. and Mrs. Bird, who are very charitable and decide to hatch the egg as if it were their own. After they give it a lot of love and care, one day it hatches. To their surprise, their adopted child is a very strange-looking bird, with a long green snout and sharp teeth—they've just hatched a baby alligator. Do they discard this dangerous predator? No, they raise it as their own.

Something similar to Mr. and Mrs. Bird's story often occurs with dream incubation; you don't always get what you asked for. When you ask your dream a question, don't expect a clear-cut answer. For example, if your question is "Should I go to law school?" don't expect your dream necessarily to answer back, "Sure, sounds like a good plan, I recommend Harvard."

When you put a question to your dreams, you often get an answer that's full of symbols and codes. It seems as if your dream is trying to tell you something, but what? In order to crack the code, the ancient Egyptians would enlist the help of a dream priest. These days, many of us consult dream dictionaries, which often lead us in the wrong direction. Dream dictionaries provide generic definitions for various symbols, but your symbols are anything but generic. They're very personal to you and your experiences.

It's understandable to be frustrated with this coded language—why won't my dream just speak in plain English? It's not that your subconscious is trying to confuse or torture you. Here's one way to think of it: The message that your dream is conveying to you cannot be summarized in specific language. Perhaps your subconscious provides you with metaphorical experiences (dreams) in order to communicate with you on a deeper level. It's up to you to interpret your own dreams. What does your gut tell you?

So you may find yourself incubating a bird until CRACK, there's an alligator. Don't be upset when you don't receive the exact dream you were hoping for. Your subconscious is answering your question, just not in the way you expected. It's smarter than you are, and may in fact be answering the question that you *should* have asked.

Summary

- Incubation is a way to decide what dream you are going to have before you have it.

- It's a millennia-old skill that dreamers have always used to find guidance and healing.

- All it takes is a passionate, specific, visual intention.

- Use incubation to set the stage for a lucid dream.

- Don't expect your dream to give a clear-cut answer to your questions.

WILD

Consciousness can be trained to leave the physical body.

—His Holiness the Dalai Lama,
one of the world's greatest spiritual leaders,
in his fourteenth reincarnation as of this writing

We've already taught you how to become lucid in your dreams using the most typical technique. The DILD, a lucid dream that's sparked by a spontaneous realization, is how 72 percent of lucid dreams happen (see page 100). Hopefully you've already had some success with that technique, and if you haven't, we're sure you will soon enough.

But what about the other 28 percent of lucid dreams? There are other ways to become lucid, and this chapter is dedicated to a second and more exotic induction technique. It's a method that's a bit more difficult to master, but the results are powerful and potentially life-changing. Shamans and yogis have practiced this approach for thousands of years.

It is dawn. I am woken up by a text. Seeing this as a good time to do a wake-back-to-bed, I go back to sleep thinking, "Okay, the next place I'll be will be a dream." I close my eyes and stare at the blankness in front of me. I can feel my body is tired, and it has begun to feel very heavy. After a couple of minutes, I can feel myself even more relaxed, almost numb. I begin hearing sounds. Every so often I hear "wisps" that sound sort of like air pressure from a teakettle. I simply observe this and focus on the darkness ahead. Waiting for an image to appear, I remind myself that the next image I'll see will be a dream. Again, I hear the sound. This time it's loud and intense. I must be close. Next thing I know, I feel as if I'm moving. My body feels like it's being lifted up and moved back and forth across the bed. I wait to open my eyes. I don't want to prematurely wake up and start over. I tell myself to remain calm and go with it. If I wait this out, I'll be in a lucid dream before I know it. The movement stops and I open my eyes. I'm turned completely around on my bed. Did I make it, am I dreaming? I jump and float up to the ceiling. Jackpot. I'm in. —THOMAS P.

Once you get a grip on it, you will be able to have a lucid dream virtually at will, whenever you want. This technique was coined and perfected by Stephen LaBerge and is called the "Wake-Initiated Lucid Dream," or WILD for short.

WILDs differ from other lucid dreams in one very important way: They require one to go from the waking state directly into a lucid dream without any lapse in consciousness. Yes, you heard right, it's possible to watch your body go to sleep while your mind remains awake and aware. This direct entry into a dream is one of the most unique and unusual experiences you may have as a lucid dreamer, or as a human for that matter. While we aren't fans of boring acronyms, the name aptly describes what this experience is like: wild. Never thought something like this was possible? Well, it's very real, and you're about to find out how to do it.

What Is a WILD Exactly?

The idea behind a WILD is simple. You want your mind to stay awake while your body falls asleep. In other words, you want to fall asleep consciously. This awesome feat boils down to one simple idea: allowing your body to relax completely while preserving a clear awareness.

This transition provides a direct entry into a lucid dream. Awake only minutes before, you can walk through the doorway of your dreams just like you'd commute to work. There is no need to become lucid with this technique, since your awareness never left in the first place.

Remember that lucidity is a spectrum, not an on-and-off switch. Typically, WILDs contain a very high level of lucidity—they are very stable and long, allowing you full, conscious influence over your inner landscape.

The Experience

Your first WILD might be intense or even scary. You may hear sounds, feel strange bodily sensations like buzzing or "vibrations," see flashes of images, or even hallucinations while crossing over the threshold between waking and dreaming. These are completely natural, don't worry. If you've ever been to a Pink Floyd concert, you already have an idea what it's like.

So how do you fall asleep consciously?

The Twilight Zone

Every day the sun sets, and just before the world gets dark we experience a transition between day and night. Dusk is a time when the physical world gives way to shadows and introspection, and the same goes for sleep, in the state that lucid dreamers know as the twilight zone. No, this isn't the 1960s TV classic, this is the place between sleeping and waking, what the French call *dorveille*. It is the springboard to WILDs.

As we lie in bed at night, neither completely asleep nor entirely awake, we experience hallucinatory images, shapes, sounds, colors, and ideas. According to Russian physicist Arkady Migdal, this intermediate state, "where consciousness and unconsciousness mix," is the optimal state for creativity.

With the logical, analytical faculties of our everyday mind temporarily shut down, the twilight zone allows for the free-flowing of images, creative connections, and intuitive impressions to rise to the surface. In fact, this fluid state has been used by many great thinkers

SHAMANS, YOGIS, AND OTHER MYSTICS

WILDs remind us what shamans have been telling us for centuries. We don't have to sleep in order to dream. For them, accessing the spirit realm is a matter of simply shifting awareness. Shamans think that our souls exist on many levels of reality, which run parallel and simultaneous to the physical world. They believe that we have access to these realms at any time simply by shifting our attention. For them, a WILD is a direct path into the dream world. One in which they can enter any time they please.

and mystics throughout history. Robert Moss calls this the "solution state," based on the countless scientific discoveries and break-throughs, all made during the cusp between sleeping and waking.

Einstein was said to use this special state to receive visuals, which helped him develop ideas. In 1905, he descended into twilight and returned with the theory of relativity whirling around in his head. Niels Bohr, the physicist who won the Nobel Prize for his model of the structure of the atom, saw in a vision the nucleus of an atom, with the electrons spinning around it, much like our solar system with the sun and planets.

Shamans, Tibetan yogis, and mystics knew the importance of this borderline zone as the springboard to receive intuitive visions or travel to other realities. They understood this liminal state to be highly conducive to psychic abilities. If you are at all interested in things like intuition, telepathy, clairvoyance, or other "subtle" abilities, then the twilight zone is your playground.

Most of the time when we sleep, we fly right past the twilight zone. Within a minute of hitting the pillow, we often conk out like a kid in a stroller after a long day at Disney World. Learning to spend more time in the twilight state, advises Robert Moss, is the best way to consciously dream. "If you can develop the ability to enter and remain in a state of relaxed, free-flowing awareness, images will come," says Moss.

How to Perform a WILD

You'll notice that the beginning steps to the WILD technique are similar to a normal lucid dream. The wake-back-to-bed, for instance, is important when attempting any kind of technique. The logic is the same: Catching your last REM cycle will thrust you directly into a dream. It will also be useful to obtain a state of almost hypnotic relaxation. Have a fun and playful attitude! The more you try to force this induction, the harder it becomes. You can't force relaxation, and this isn't the time to be competitive.

Simply allow your body to do what it naturally does already—go to sleep. A WILD doesn't require you to do much more than to sit back and enjoy the show.

Preparation: Wake-Back-to-Bed

1. Set your alarm. Catch your last REM cycle by setting your alarm clock one to two hours before you would normally wake up.

2. Wake up. Awaken for fifteen to twenty minutes. Same as before. Read, go to the bathroom, knit yourself a sweater, do a

multiplication problem. Get your mind awake but move slowly and keep your body relaxed.

REM ATONIA

REM atonia is your body's way of protecting you from yourself. As you enter REM, your body becomes physiologically paralyzed. Nature built in this nifty function to protect you from acting out your dreams. In short, the body shuts itself off so that it cannot move while you dream. If we were able to move, we'd probably have people jumping out of windows thinking they could fly, playing the marimba on their kitchen counters, and punching their sleeping partners. Thanks, REM atonia! You'd think that sleepwalking is related to atonia, but you'd be wrong. Sleepwalking occurs during non-REM sleep.

Relaxation

3. Lie back down. Now focus on your breath and let go of any tension you might be holding in your body. Feel how comfortable your bed feels. Focus your awareness on the blackness in front of you, but don't get caught up in your thoughts. Simply let them drift in and out. The trick here is finding a balance between a relaxed body and an alert mind. Stephen LaBerge calls this a state of attentive relaxation.

Transition

4. Hypnagogic imagery. As you transition through the twilight zone into the dream world, you should begin to see random streaks of color or flashes of light dancing beneath your closed eyelids. Sometimes they take the form of images with no story, like flipping through different TV channels. This is the beginning of the hypnagogic imagery, something we all experience as we fall asleep each day. Congratulations, you're almost asleep!

5. Deepening. Your body will begin feeling heavy or numb. Your senses of the outside world will begin to diminish, and you might feel other sensations like buzzing or vibrations. This is the onset of REM atonia, a very natural state that your body goes into each time you dream. Basically, your body is physically paralyzed, but your mind is still awake. You're only seconds away! Watch the images in front of you until one becomes very clear. This one, clear image should stay there in front of you for a couple seconds and eventually move toward you (or you toward it). It will engulf you.

6. Jackpot. You're in! Congratulations. You have just entered a lucid dream directly from the waking world. Remind yourself that you're dreaming and explore your surroundings. Talk with dream characters, fly, write a poem, create a beach house, seek answers to an important life question, or simply sit back and relish your awareness.

Tips on WILD

🐝 **Relax.** Your body knows what to do. If you're having trouble falling back to sleep, it might be because you're thinking too much. An alert mind is not necessarily a thinking mind. Try to clear your head and have a passive awareness. Imagine that you're watching a great movie and enjoy the show.

🐝 **Don't move.** Moving your body will just lengthen the process. Focus on releasing all tension and feel how comfortable your bed is.

🐝 **Hands up.** If you are falling asleep too quickly and losing awareness, try this: Lift your forearm perpendicular to your upper arm like it's in a cast. As you drift off to sleep, your arm will naturally fall back to the bed and serve as a reminder of your goal. Repeat this step if necessary. Your body will fall asleep within seconds.

🐝 **Keep a focused mind.** This can be challenging. Continuously remind yourself of your intention as your body turns off. Try counting. "One . . . I'm dreaming . . . two . . . I'm dreaming . . . three . . . I'm dreaming . . ." This will help focus your mind while your body does its thing.

🐝 **Be careful of false awakenings.** A common phenomenon known as a false awakening occurs when you mistakenly think you're awake, when you're actually surrounded by a very realistic dream. Personally, we've been sitting in bed, writing in our dream journals and apparently awake, only to wake up again and see the page blank! Always perform a reality check and make sure. Are you dreaming?

Summary

- If you want to have a lucid dream at will, learn how to perform a WILD.

- A WILD involves falling asleep consciously, letting your body fall asleep while you, that is your consciousness, remains aware.

- Practice spending time in the twilight state: It's the springboard to your lucid dreams.

- Relax and let your body do what it normally does while you focus passively on the images ahead of you. Wait until one of the images becomes clear and move toward it.

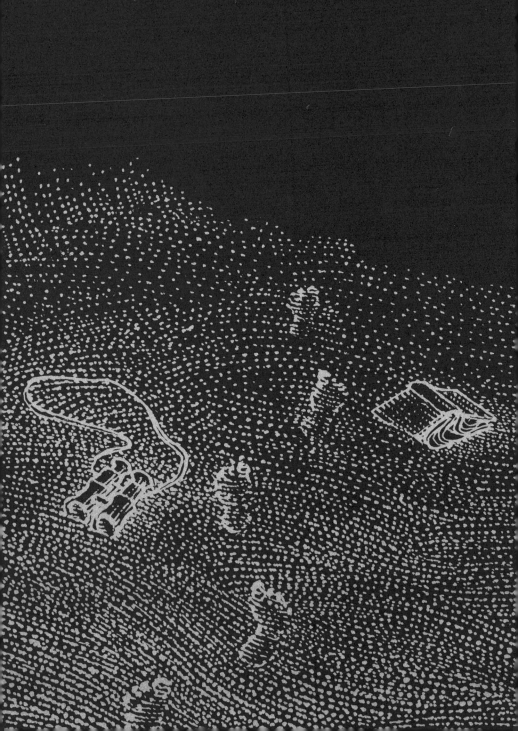

PART SIX

THE NEXT
FRONTIER

W elcome to the end. You've been to a lot of places and have seen many things. But wait—don't unpack your bags, don't let down those sails, you've only just begun. As the captain you can take control of your ship and venture further into a world of limitless possibilities. There are places to uncover, things to do, ideas to experiment with, and discoveries to be made.

When we first set sail to the dream world, we were like freshmen at a college mixer. There was flying, anonymous dream sex, fireball battles, and all-around good fun. We're not ashamed of these activities. Once the limits of the waking world were lifted, there were just some things that we had to try. Biting our thumbs at gravity, seducing jungle harpies, and traveling into space were all liberating experiences.

Then sophomore year rolled around and we turned to lucid dreaming to help with our waking-life problems. The practices of defusing nightmares and incubating dreams enriched our lives and made us feel more whole. Our journey went from fun to profound.

Then it was time to graduate. It was time to go beyond the personal into the transpersonal. We took a break from being entertained and ventured out into the unknown. As we traveled toward the horizon, our viewpoints and philosophies were challenged.

Now we invite you to explore the bigger picture. Let's probe the true nature of dreams. Let's learn more about ourselves. The dream world and the waking world seem like completely different realities; let's examine how these two worlds intersect. We'll see how lucid dreaming could change our entire culture and society.

So far, we've gone on a lot about how to dream, but maybe the more important question is why we dream.

19

Know Thyself

~·~

It is wisdom to know others;
it is enlightenment to know one's self.

—Lao-tzu,
writer, philosopher, incredible beard

The Journey

Legends, myths, and stories of old tell of a hero's quest to master and overcome challenges, to find the treasure, or save the town from peril. But the classic journeys are not just entertaining. As Saint Catherine of Siena said, "Heroes take journeys, confront dragons, and discover the treasure of their true selves." You are the hero in your life's story, and your journey will take you to the greatest treasure of all: self-discovery.

The Royal Road to Your Unconscious

"The interpretation of dreams is the royal road to a knowledge of the unconscious activities of the mind." When Freud said this, he was speaking about a deep part of the human psyche. He was convinced that there is some deeper part of ourselves that contains our repressed memories, underlying thoughts, beliefs, and emotions. We are unaware of this place, but it still influences our actions and feelings in waking life. Freud believed the role of psychotherapy was to uncover this "unconscious" and bring it to light. By integrating the conscious mind with the subconscious mind we can radically transform our lives, he thought.

Why do we act a certain way? Why do we sometimes find ourselves in recurring situations or circumstances? What are the internal blocks that keep us from living life fully? Our lives are sculpted by our internal worlds. But if we are simply a product of our imaginations and all that hidden stuff, how do we take control? If only there was some tool to uncover our own hidden thoughts and feelings.

You know what we're getting at here. Dreams can act as a mirror to our subconscious minds. When we look back on a dream the morning after, we are taking a peek at our inner life. Swirling in our heads we see habits, thoughts, fears, and recurring patterns, coded in the language of the dream. By seeing these elements, and bringing them into our awareness, we're pulling them out of our subconscious and introducing them into our conscious minds. As Freud's successor Carl Jung stated, "Man's task is to become conscious of the contents that press upward from the unconscious."

Looking within and exploring our inner universe is a way to learn more about ourselves and become whole, believed Jung. We couldn't agree more.

Sure, regular dreams can definitely reveal some interesting things going on within you, but what about lucid dreaming? With self-reflective awareness in the dream state, we can communicate directly with the vast landscape of our minds. While lucid, we're able to engage with what many people call the Self (aka the higher self, the subconscious self, God, the soul, the Universe—call it what you will).

Lucid dreams can lead to incredible insights. They can help you find your way along this crazy path of life. Next time you find yourself conscious inside a dream, ask some questions and make use of the vast wisdom of your own subconscious. Here are some tips:

🐝 **Look for a guide/spirit animal.** It doesn't matter if it's an animal, a person, or a paper airplane. Whatever form it takes, an ally can be a great help when exploring your inner world. Pose questions to your guide or ask it to take you to a meaningful location.

🐝 **Interpret the dream *inside the dream*.** You don't have to wait until you wake up to interpret your dream. Think of your subconscious as a wise old man, your own personal Mr. Miyagi. Ask the dream for insights and then observe what your subconscious reveals to you, interpreting the events and characters of your dream as they unfold. A great thing to say once lucid is, "Show me what I need to know," and sit back and observe. Use your intuition to interpret the dream. Make it a stress-free, creative endeavor.

🐝 **Think outside the box.** Don't be shy—quit twiddling your thumbs and ask the big questions. Examine your own beliefs of space, time, intuition, and awareness, and then challenge those beliefs, if only for fun. Don't be afraid of sounding like a mustachioed philosophy major either. Ponder the existential puzzles like:

- Who am I?
- Where am I?
- What is God?
- What are time and space?
- Am I my body?
- What does my soul look like?
- What the hell happens when I die?

These questions are classics for a reason.

🐝 **Observe the dream environment.** The location you find your-self in is a reflection of you. You can observe and even engage with the elements of the dream that surround you to learn more about your inner workings. Do you find yourself on a busy city street, near a peaceful lake, in a familiar home, per-haps? The environment you find yourself in during a dream is no accident. If, for example, you find yourself in a house, explore the different rooms. Take note of the decor, the upkeep of the house, or even the size of the space itself.

Walk upstairs and explore the attic; maybe you'll find some lofty ideas. Venture underground to the basement and seek out hidden memories. Don't just stand there, engage your environment and ask it to reveal its secrets to you.

Mirror, Mirror

The day came when the risk to remain tight in a bud
was more painful than the risk it took to blossom.

—Anaïs Nin,
French-Cuban author, one of the finest writers of erotica

⌒⌐•⌐⌒

Just as we look into a mirror to get dressed, to check our hair, or to pop a pimple, our dreams are a tool for us to see our own reflections. On a superficial level, we may look into a mirror on some mornings and notice that we look like crap. That may compel us to shower, shave, change our clothes, etc. Without the mirror, we wouldn't know how to change. Likewise, what happens when we look into our dreams and find ourselves distorted in ways that we don't find attractive? "Why did I beat that old lady to a pulp in my dream?" you ask. "What does that say about me?"

There may be some aspects of your inner reflection that you won't like. Don't worry if you discover these things. That's the whole point of the dream, to raise your present level of awareness. The beauty is that once you see something and are aware of it, you can change it. Abraham Maslow understood this idea when he said, "What is necessary to change a person is to change his awareness of himself." What are your dreams about and how do they make you feel? What could they be trying to tell you? The experiences you have within the dream can be a very personal wake-up call.

Like a mirror, lucid dreaming is simply a tool we can use to examine the limiting beliefs or subconscious tendencies that might be holding us back. In one way or another, we're all on a journey to find out who we are. Lucid dreaming can be used to reconnect with our past selves, to find out our true purpose, to tap into deep wisdom, and to learn more about this strange thing we call reality. Armed with this knowledge, you'll move forward in life with conviction.

No matter what your journey is, what your religion is, where or how you grew up, dream exploration can be a way to understand who you truly are.

Summary

- Make the conscious choice to pay attention to your inner life. This involves your dreams, thoughts, feelings, and any subconscious beliefs you hold.

- Peer into a dream as if you're looking into a mirror and reflect upon what you see. The more awareness you have of yourself, the more deliberate you can be with your thoughts and actions.

- Lucid dreaming provides us with a unique opportunity to explore our inner selves consciously and to seek knowledge or guidance once we're there.

- With lucid dreaming we can begin merging our subconscious with our conscious minds, thus revealing and understanding more about ourselves.

20

Waking vs. Dreaming

*Thoughts are things, and powerful things at that, when they are
mixed with definiteness of purpose, persistence, and a burning desire.*

—Napoleon Hill,
successful writer who wrote about success

While writing this book, our experiences with lucid dreaming sparked a shift in our realities. Our lives became significantly altered—not just our dream lives, but our day-to-day lives as well. Experiences in the dream world forced us to ask some curious questions: What is the relationship between the physical world and the dream world? Can the lessons and principles we learned as lucid dreamers apply to our waking lives? What can dreams, and specifically the lucid dream experience, tell us about ourselves and the world?

As we explored these puzzles we found that there are indeed a lot of correlations between dreaming and waking. We think these connections will be helpful to anyone who's looking to improve his or her daily life. In this chapter we'll take a look at a few of these correlations.

We Are All Together

Sure. We've all heard this before. We're all one. We get it. Yet in the dream state, this lofty philosophical idea is something that you can actually experience. In dreams, everything, from a rock to a feather to a dream character, is imbued with a consciousness. Everything is you and you feel this intimate connection. Even the air around you, the space between things, feels like it is alive and conscious. How else do you think you could conjure up an object or a dream character out of thin air? We don't mean this philosophically. In the dream world, everything is connected.

What about the real world then?

The story at left is amazing, but what's even more amazing is that Jordan had this experience in the waking world. We might expect to feel a personal connection to everything in our own dreams, but when we have those same moments of clarity while we're awake, it feels as though there's a vast web connecting everything.

This idea is no secret. Spiritual masters and mystics have told us for centuries that everything is more closely

I was standing on a roof and looking at a cityscape. I had a wave of clarity rush over me, and the world around me and myself seemed to expand. I was able to understand my place in the bigger picture and felt in deep connection with the universe around me. I was in a relationship with everything—even the air around me felt embedded with this very intimate presence, which was my own. I felt like I was both creator and observer of my entire world. I felt empowered as chills and vibrations went through my entire being. It was truly incredible and brought me to the point of tears. —JORDAN F.

connected than our physical boundaries would seem to suggest. Everything looks separate, of course. There is me and then there is you and there's a dog and there's a couch. All separate. But throughout time, many religions and even some scientists today will tell you that separation is an illusion.

The most astounding fact is the knowledge that the atoms that comprise life on Earth, the atoms that make up the human body, are traceable to the crucibles that cooked light elements into heavy elements in their core under extreme temperatures and pressures. These stars—the high mass ones among them went unstable—in their later years they collapsed and then exploded, scattering their enriched guts across the galaxy. Guts made of carbon, nitrogen, oxygen, and all the fundamental ingredients of life itself. So that when I look up at the night sky and I know that yes, we are part of this universe, we are in this universe, but perhaps more important than both of those facts is that the universe is in us. When I reflect on that fact, I look up—many people feel small because they're small and the universe is big—but I feel big, because my atoms came from those stars. There's a level of connectivity.

—Neil deGrasse Tyson,
astrophysicist, director of the Hayden Planetarium, cosmic celebrity

So we're connected to everything else in existence—each other, nature, and the big ol' universe. It's a nice idea, but how does one feel connected to the universe on a regular basis? Do we have to meditate in a cave for thirty years and become enlightened to feel this? Do we have to take drugs and "trip out" every time we see a flower? Do we even need to have a lucid dream every night? Many of us don't have the time or affinity for all that.

Let's refer to our friend Abraham Maslow. He believed that if we look at only what's psychologically wrong with us, we won't get the full picture of who we are. Maslow performed a radical psychological study: He looked at individuals with great mental health instead of people with serious psychological issues.

What was so interesting about these acclaimed "self-actualizers" was that they frequently experienced what he called "peak experiences," high points in life when the individual was in harmony with himself and his surroundings. These moments were often accompanied by intense clarity, feelings of ecstasy, wholeness, and a connection to the world. The average person may experience a few of these moments spontaneously throughout his lifetime, but according to Maslow these self-actualizers were able to have peak experiences daily.

How do you become a self-actualized person? It's easier said than done. You can't force a peak experience after all. While we don't have a road map to experiencing the world as a connected web of cosmic beauty, a good place to start is to take what you've learned from the dream world and apply it to your waking life. In other words, to live lucidly.

WALKING AROUND IN A DREAM

The next time you're out and about in the world, imagine that you're dreaming and that everything and everyone is really just a part of you. Like the dream world you've come to know so well, pretend that you're surrounded by your own internal landscape.

Lucid Living

Let's wake up! Let's wake up in our relationships,
let's wake up where we work, let's wake up in where we live.

—Fariba Bogzaran, PhD,
artist, dream researcher, writer

Have you ever driven to work only to pull into the parking lot with the puzzled and anxious realization "How did I just get here?" With little recollection of the fifteen-minute drive, you wonder, "Did I stop at traffic lights? Was I speeding?"

Your memory draws a blank.

Some of us go through the motions of life automatically. We fill our days with routines and errands. Our buzzing minds are anxious about the future or regretful about the past. We let others dictate our reality, letting life chug on by like a runaway train.

It's as if we're in a dream, wandering aimlessly in a kind of sleepy trance.

They who dream by day are cognizant of many things
which escape those who dream at night.

—Edgar Allan Poe,
macabre American poet, fan of ravens

The goal of lucid dreaming is not to sleep away your life, but to bring this increased awareness into your everyday existence. When we learn to become lucid in our lives, we become more aware of our surroundings, more aware of our reality and how we are engaging with it, shaping it, communicating with it. Being lucid in the waking world means being mindful of your actions, decisions, and choices. It means being so vividly engaged with life that anything that came before seems like a hazy dream.

Tenzin Rinpoche, in his book *The Tibetan Yogas of Dream and Sleep,* describes a truth that's at the center of Tibetan Dream Yoga: "The dynamics of a dream are easier to understand in a dream, because they can be observed free of the limitations of the physical world and the rational consciousness. During the day, although still engaged in the same dream-making process, we project this inner activity of the mind onto the world and think that our experiences are 'real' and external to our own mind."

We've all had the cynical friend who complains about everything, even on the good days. Or that chipper person at work who is bursting with excitement about every little thing. This world can be a nightmare or a nice dream. It's full of friends or enemies, success or failure, meaning or nihilism. We're headed toward destruction or we're headed toward rebirth. There are as many viewpoints on Earth as there are people. And just like the dream, we shape our experience with our thoughts, emotions, and expectations.

Having awareness while awake and in your dreams allows you to deliberately steer yourself on your path through life. As you bring more awareness into your life you will:

• Be less and less governed by habits and routines.
• Learn how to bring intention into your life.

- Take life more symbolically and dreams more literally.
- Clearly see the everyday patterns you fall into.
- Go about creating the world you want to live in.

THE DOUBLE SLIT EXPERIMENT

Thomas Young, a scientist in the early 1800s, shot an electron toward a wall with two slits in it. What he discovered was this: An electron sent toward a plate with two parallel slits close to each other passes through both simultaneously. Depending on how Young observed the electron, it would behave either as a particle behaves or like a wave. The idea surprised everyone: By just observing something you can change it. With recent discoveries in quantum physics, science and math are now building on the double slit experiment, discovering just how much our perception creates reality. We now know that Young's experiment is a result of the phenomenon of quantum superposition, which is a fancy way of saying that an electron is in all possible locations at the same time. Instead of a rigid path that an electron is forced to follow, there is a field of possibilities. As we start to peer into the building blocks of matter, looking at electrons and quarks, we can see that matter is made up of 99 percent empty space, with tiny tiny charged particles floating around. That's right, the world only seems solid because of these charged particles, but at a quantum level there seems to be only energy, nothing solid at all. While these notions might scare some of us, we oneironauts get a kick out of them: They suggest that the world is much more malleable than it seems, and that our consciousness creates, shapes, and affects the world around us, just like a dream.

SPIRIT GUIDES

Historically, the term "spirit guide" generally refers to one or more entities who protect, teach, and heal you on your physical journey into spiritual awareness. The idea pops up in many cultures. It's believed that an individual may have more than one spirit guide, and a guide may change over the course of someone's lifetime. These beings are here to help us when we are in turmoil or seeking assistance.

Incubating Reality

If it's true that we create our realities, that gives us a lot of power, doesn't it? That means our thoughts, feelings, and actions are now in our control. If that's true, then it's possible to claim ownership over our own lives and steer our ships toward peaceful horizons.

From the beginning, we've been preaching about the idea of "juice" or passion. If you want to incubate a dream, or create anything in the dream world, that desire needs to have passion behind it.

If you find this to be true while lucid dreaming, why not try the same technique after you wake up? Need to wash your car, find a new job, or ask that cute boy out at the bookstore? Having a specific, focused, and passionate intention will do wonders.

When you know what you want, it will be a lot easier to obtain it.

MONKS AND DREAMERS BATTLE IT OUT

Brain waves are simply the measurement of the brain's electrical activity. When we're going about our normal, day-to-day lives, our brain waves are in beta, measured at 12 to 30 Hz. Theta waves (4 to 8 Hz) take over our brains while we're slipping into twilight, and they continue pulsing as we dream. Recently, scientists have been looking at a rare kind of brain wave, gamma, which is measured at 25 to 100 Hz. In a 2004 study, scientist Richard Davidson studied the brains of nearly a dozen monks, generously referred to him by the Dalai Lama. Davidson hooked these monks up to an EEG and, when he asked them to meditate on "compassion," they produced brain waves in the 25 to 30 Hz range—gamma waves! Fast-forward to 2009, Frankfurt University. Six participants were monitored as they slept. The six had recently been trained in a four-month course on how to lucid dream. As they became conscious in their dreams, the machines lit up: The novice lucid dreamers reached gamma, their brains peaking at 40 Hz cycles per minute, higher than the Dalai Lama's best meditators!

Of course, in the waking world, getting what you want is a bit tougher than in your dreams. In your lucid dreams, the only thing that stands between a desire and the fulfillment of that desire is yourself. Is that true of the waking world? Yes and no.

The waking world is full of concrete issues, real solid obstacles that stand in your way. Let's say you want to start a career as a doctor. You'd have to find money for medical school, go through several years of school, start a practice, etc.

These hurdles do exist, but they're not necessarily problems, not if you don't perceive them in that way. Again, you are in control of how you see the world, and if you choose to be stressed-out and discouraged by obstacles, they will turn into frightening trolls, blocking the way to your goal.

If you keep your intention clearly in mind, and choose to see obstacles as inevitable but surpassable facts of life, the frightening trolls will shrink into small kittens of inconsequence.

The Lucid Hangover

A common question we're asked is, "If you master lucid dreaming, what makes you want to return to reality?" Reality can be boring. If dreams are a landscape of your own creation, won't you become disappointed when you have to return to your day-to-day life?

What is the cure to the lucid dream hangover?

The goal is to never be disappointed by reality. Most lucid dreamers will tell you that the lucid hangover doesn't exist, and in fact the opposite occurs. Upon waking, many feel a joyful, warm buzz.

As you return from your dreams, take everything back with you. That rush you got while flying, those tears you shed when you talked with your deceased grandmother, the feeling of pride and confidence when you fought off that nightmarish demon, and most important, beyond anything else, the feeling of clarity you got from being awake.

Know that you are the dreamer of your life, and just like a lucid dream you can change the way you experience reality at any moment. Like your trusty compass, its silver needle always pointing north, your lucidity should stay with you at all times.

Summary

The principles we learned in the dream world can be applied to our waking experience as well.

- In a lucid dream, we can experience the philosophical idea of "we are all one."

- Your thoughts, emotions, and expectations shape your dream life. These things have a strong creative power in your waking life as well.

- What if you could sculpt your waking life just like you can sculpt a dream? How could the principles you learned in the dream world, such as "change yourself, not the dream" apply to your waking life?

A Future Vision

~—•—~

The future belongs to those who believe in the beauty of their dreams.

—Eleanor Roosevelt,
civil rights activist, first lady, all-around kick-ass woman

The human species has been growing and maturing since we awoke on the grassy savanna some 150,000 years ago. The evolutionary leap that ultimately separated us from our predecessors wasn't a physical change, it was an internal one. It was the emergence of self-reflective consciousness—in other words, we became aware that we were aware. This made us into a unique species. Prior to this radical change, humans walked around the waking world much like we walk around in our dreams today—void of self-reflection in a sort of automatic, reactive state. Before this change, we were aware of our external environment, sure, but we didn't have the ability to reflect upon life. After the change, we emerged as *Homo sapiens sapiens,* Latin for "man wise

wise," or, as author Michael Mahoney muses, "he who knows he knows." We were human beings, equipped with an enlarged perspective and an internal world.

Grab hold of your hats, we may be on the brink of another evolutionary leap. Like that paradigm shift so long ago, this change would not be a physical one. We won't grow a new tail or learn how to spit venom out of our mouths.

What if today's change is an internal one as well? What if we are awakening, only this time within the internal landscapes of our minds?

In the average dream, we walk around without any capacity for self-reflection. We interact with the dream as if it's real life. While our waking minds have evolved for thousands of years, it's as though our dreaming brain is still stuck on autopilot, void of the same cognitive abilities we possess during our waking hours. What if lucid dreaming is the beginning of another evolutionary development? The emergence of a new capacity for self-awareness?

So far this field guide has focused on YOU: your adventure, your problems. Don't get us wrong, you're great, you really are. But let's pull back the camera and take a look at the bigger picture. What would it look like if this ability wasn't just a hobby, but a cornerstone of our societies? Could lucid dreaming change the world?

Projecting into the Future

In the history of the collective as in the history of the individual,
everything depends on the development of consciousness.

—Carl Jung
protégé of Freud, example of student becoming the master

❧ • ❧

As soon as our ancestors began to think about thinking, other things began to emerge that we now take for granted: imagination, forethought, curiosity, complex logic, reason, etc. With our new ability to self-reflect in the dream, we too could find ourselves with capacities previously unavailable to us. The world might drastically change if we simply began valuing our dreams as a real and transformative tool of experience.

Guidance

In the future, lucid dreaming could be an internal compass helping us to seek out answers to questions, both personal and collective. As in many cultures before us, the average person would be in touch with their dreams. Daily dream interpretation would provide us with guidance and insights.

In the same way that we talk about the weather with a spouse or friend, we'd discuss our dreams, both regular and lucid, on a daily basis and help each other discover the hidden meanings. We'd use the Internet to spread and share dreams like we share our waking life experiences on Facebook. You might wake up every morning and publish your dreams to a social media circle or network. The possibilities are endless.

Healing

What if the medical and mental health professions accepted the importance of lucid dreams when working with their patients? While dream work is already a practice for many psychologists and professionals around the world, we see it becoming much more accessible to the everyday person. The medical community has already accepted the practices of meditation and guided imagery, so why not also use lucid dreaming? Since the body and mind are connected, people can dramatically affect their health by working with their dreams. Lucid dreaming could be offered in conjunction with cancer treatments and therapy. Past traumas, emotional difficulties, fears, anxiety, depression, and physical ailments could all be mended within the dream world in a holistic approach. Professionals would still exist, but the average person would feel confident and empowered about taking aspects of their health into their own hands.

Education and Work

For dreaming to be integrated into our society, it must find a respectful and healthful place within our educational system. What would it look like if we encourage children to pay attention, share, and cultivate their dreaming skills? To accommodate a dreaming culture, both adults and children would make more time for dreaming. Maybe naps would become a common daily ritual. (How come only kids get nap time?) During that mid-day nap, you would sometimes conduct lucid dreaming or dream incubation techniques. You could even continue working on your education or projects in the dream world. Conscious dreaming is a

great way to tap into your creativity, solve problems, and rehearse skills such as instrument playing, public speaking, and athletics. What if our schools taught lucid dreaming and encouraged students to use dreams as a testing ground? The dream world would be a classroom of its own (but way more fun).

Creativity

All things must be imagined before they can be created. A table must first be envisioned before it can be constructed and then used. An architect uses his mind's eye and a passionate intention to design and plan a building before it can be realized physically. This is as true in the dream world as it is in the waking world. As George Bernard Shaw wrote, "Imagination is the beginning of creation. You imagine what you desire; you will what you imagine; and at last you create what you will." In a dreaming culture, dreams would be the tool of choice for encouraging creativity. We would turn our dreams into reality.

What if our society's artists could create without the limits of time, censorship, or materials? An inventor could test out an invention, a writer could create the landscape of his novel within the dream, and an executive could find the right words to use during next week's presentation. Any field could use dreaming as a tool for expanding one's creative potency. Instead of drawing a picture or sitting quietly with your imagination, what if the average person traveled to the dream world to experience the feel, weight, and details of a creation before it became tangible?

Dreaming of the Future

We must teach our children to dream with their eyes open.

—Harry Edwards,
sociologist, activist for African American athletes

What are you going to do tomorrow? Stop for a second, just a second, and think about this question. Picture your plans for tomorrow in your mind's eye. Perhaps you'll walk the dog, go to work, come home, and play with the kids. Maybe you'll give a public speech in front of an audience, win a tournament, sign a contract, fly in an airplane, or begin painting again. If you could have it your way, what would happen tomorrow?

What you just did was use your imagination to create a future that doesn't exist yet. Congrats! As far as we know, humans are the only species who have this capacity.

Think about it. Without the ability to reflect we would all be stuck doing the same thing, going around in an endless circle. We could never imagine a future that is not now, and we'd be doomed to play out old patterns and behaviors. Thanks to imagination, we are propelled into the unknown, inspired to create something new.

We create who we are through our imaginations. When someone says something like, "My dream is to own my own business," or "I dream to one day be a champion table tennis pro," they are using the word *dream* to describe an unmanifested possibility.

Our ambitions and goals are possibilities that come into existence through the process of creation.

All too often, we use our imagination to picture what we don't want. We envisage all of our worst fears, all the things that could go wrong in a situation. We end up paralyzed by doubts before we've even started. In a dreaming society, however, we could use the power of imagination for good, rather than for evil.

It seems that our world is experiencing a crisis on many fronts. Whether it's environmental, political, economical, social, or educational, the world is going through a bit of a rough patch. As we think about solutions to our global problems, could dreaming be added near the top of the list?

If we're going to create a better world, first we have to dream it into existence. We're already involved in this process of creation, it's just that we do it unconsciously. Sure, fixing our planet will take action and innovation. But why not become aware of this process that's going on under the radar, grab the wheel, and steer in a better direction?

In other words, in order to change the world, we must change ourselves.

Why Do We Dream?

We are not solid beings. We are without limits.

—Don Juan,
as written by Carlos Castaneda

~ • ~

It takes the tiniest of steps through the thin film of the unknown to see what's on the other side. A world to explore. A world to understand. If there were no divers to drop through the surface of the ocean, we would be oblivious of the wonders of the sea. If we had never blasted through the upper atmosphere of our planet, we wouldn't know about the huge vastness of space. A quick peek behind the curtains of our dreams and we can see that the landscape stretches on to infinity.

Curiosity has propelled us humans through a rich history of discovery. The mysteries of the universe continue to nudge us into new territories, whetting our appetite for the unknown. Many questions have been asked, many more will be asked, and the common thread between them boils down to one simple word: *Why?*

So why do we dream?

Dreams can be so powerful, so uplifting, so indescribably profound and life-changing that we wake up feeling different or changed in some way. We can do our greatest work in our dreams. We can find answers, overcome limitations and fears, explore new possibilities, unlock creativity, find healing, love, wholeness. The experiences we have at night, whether we remember them or not, influence us in more ways than we can imagine.

When we awaken inside a lucid dream, we catch a glimpse of our reflections. We look around at the epic nature of our true selves and the world around us. We realize that we are, in fact, much more than our physical bodies. We reach beyond the edges of the waking world and see that reality exists on more levels than the physical. That we have the capacity to function and experience within these other worlds with complete awareness. We realize that we are, in essence, boundless creators with the imagination and the power to change our dreams, our lives, our minds, and our future.

Here it is, the end. But don't worry, don't despair. With the end of one journey comes the start of another. A true pioneer never stops exploring. Finding one world is just the bridge into discovering the next. As you prepare for your next adventure, call upon the tools and techniques you've picked up throughout this book. We hope they serve you well. As we go our separate ways, remember to keep your excitement high and your spirit strong. Be bold as you set out toward the horizon.

Sweet dreams.

NOTES

CHAPTER 1: *A New Discovery*

4   *keep breathing, and the eyes* Carl DeGuzman and Kevin Morton, "REM Sleep—Exploring a Fascinating Sleep State," 2010, End-Your-Sleep-Deprivation.com, accessed December 26, 2011, http://www.end-your-sleep-deprivation.com/rem-sleep.html.

5   *in fact dreaming and doing so consciously* *Tenth Anniversary Issue of Lucidity Letter,* ed., Elinor Gebremedhin, 10th ed. (San Francisco: Lucidity Association, 1991), 303.

5   *from another solar system in space* Keith Hearne, *The Dream Machine: Lucid Dreams and How to Control Them* (Wellingborough, U.K.: Aquarian Press, 1990).

10   *at least one lucid dream in their lifetime* R. Stepansky, B. Holzinger, A. Schmeiser-Rieder, B. Saletu, M. Kunze, and J. Zeitlhofer, "Austrian Dream Behavior: Results of a Representative Population Survey," *Dreaming* 8 (1998): 23–30.

10   *or introverted, you can become lucid* M. Schredl and D. Erlacher, "Lucid Dreaming Frequency and Personality," *Personality and Individual Differences* 37 (2004): 1463–73.

11   *having sex with the first girl I can find* Xan Brooks, "'It's Complexicated,'" *Guardian .co.uk,* February 13, 2007, http://www.guardian.co.uk/film/2007/feb/14/1.

14   *seems on the verge of becoming much better known* Stephanie Rosenbloom, "Living Your Dreams, in a Manner of Speaking," *New York Times,* September 16, 2007.

CHAPTER 2: *What Are Dreams?*

18   *the gist of her advice* "Paul McCartney and Barry Miles," *Paul McCartney: Many Years from Now* (London: Vintage, 1998).

18   *works of art, and many other discoveries* Gary Gardner, "Incredible Famous Dreams," *Lucid Dream Lessons Blog,* March 4, 2009, http://www.luciddreamlessons .com/2009/03/04/incredible-famous-dreams/.

19   *wrote Jack Kerouac* Jack Kerouac, *Book of Dreams* (San Francisco: City Lights Books, 2001).

19   *for about two hours each night* Adam Schneider and G. William Domhoff, "Dreams: FAQ." *The Quantitative Study of Dreams,* University of California, Santa Cruz, September 2011, http://www2.ucsc.edu/dreams/FAQ/index.html.

20   *mental, emotional, and physical well-being* Kendra Cherry, "Why Do We Dream? Top Dream Theories," About.com Psychology, September 2011, http://psychology.about .com/od/statesofconsciousness/p/dream-theories.htm.

21   *and ready to process more information* C. Evans and E. Newman, "Dreaming: An Analogy from Computers," *New Scientist* (1964): 577–79.

21 *prepare and practice for upcoming events* Ernest Hartmann, "Making Connections in a Safe Place: Is Dreaming Psychotherapy?," *Dreaming* 6 (1996): 213–28.

21 *biological processes that occur during sleep* J. A. Hobson, *Sleep* (New York: Scientific American Library, 1995).

21 *lobe tries to organize it into a storyline* Ibid.

22 *spent the night than an amnesiac drunk* Robert Moss, *Conscious Dreaming: A Spiritual Path for Everyday Life* (New York: Crown Trade Paperbacks, 1996), 72.

22 *dream is not the dream itself* Ibid., 64.

CHAPTER 3: *A History of Dreaming*

27 *to the realm of "spirit"* Robert Moss, *The Secret History of Dreaming* (Novato, CA: New World Library, 2009), xiv.

27 *transcended the physical world* Robert Moss, *Dreamgates: An Explorer's Guide to the Worlds of Soul, Imagination, and Life Beyond Death* (New York: Three Rivers Press, 1998), 5.

28 *not in touch with their soul* Ibid.

28 *king's decisions in the waking world* "The Epic of Gilgamesh," *SparkNotes*, March 29, 2012, http://www.sparknotes.com/lit/gilgamesh/section1.html.

29 *while the body slept* Kasia Maria Szpakowska, "The Perception of Dreams and Nightmares in Ancient Egypt: Old Kingdom to Third Intermediate Period" (dissertation, UCLA, 2000), 23–26.

29 *commonly missed in daily waking life* Lucy Gillis, "And Now a Word from Ancient Egypt . . .," *The Lucid Dream Exchange*, August 2011, http://www.dreaminglucid.com/pastldeissues.html.

29 *"Masters of the Secret Things"* Moss, *Secret History of Dreaming*, 11–12.

29 *and his son, Morpheus, ruled dreams* Dawn Firewolf, "A History Of Dreaming—From Ancient Egypt To Modern Day," *Realmagick.com* (blog), August 2011, http://www.realmagick.com/6181/a-history-of-dreaming-from-ancient-egypt-to-modern-day/.

29 *with the help of nightly dreams* Raymond L. Lee, "Forgotten Fantasies." *Dreaming* 20 (2010): 290.

30 *expression of our repressed desires* Sarah Kofman, "Mirror and Oneiric Mirages: Plato, Precursor of Freud," *The Harvard Review of Philosophy* VII (1999).

30 *which peers out in sleep* Artemidorus, *Oneirocritica: Interpretation of Dreams*, trans. Robert J. White (Torrance, CA: Original Books, Inc., 1990) 3:11.

30 *Mere coincidence* Aristotle, *On Dreams,* trans. J. I. Beare (Charlottesville, VA: InteLex, 2007).

30   *And birds resemble women* Artemidorus, *Oneirocritica,* 3:11.

30   *personal background into account* Artemidorus, *Oneirocritica.*

30   *also revived by the Romans* Carl Huffman, "Pythagoreanism" in *Stanford Encyclopedia of Philosophy,* revised June 14, 2010, ed. Edward N. Zalta, accessed March 29, 2012, http://plato.stanford.edu/entries/pythagoreanism/.

31   *all but wiped out* Raymond L. Lee, "Forgotten Fantasies." *Dreaming* 20 (2010): 291.

31   *when Vishnu's dream ends* Moss, *Secret History of Dreaming,* 51.

31   *dreaming us into existence* Ibid., 55.

31   *than the waking state* "The Oldest Language Known to Man." *School of Metaphysics.* 1995. School of Metaphysics. July 2011, http://www.som.org/1dreams/history.htm.

32   *dream beings, and shape-shifting into other animals* Rebecca Turner, "Dream Yoga: Lucid Dreaming in Tibetan Buddhism," *World of Lucid Dreaming,* July 2011, http://www.world-of-lucid-dreaming.com/dream-yoga.html.

32   *all life is but a dream* B. Alan Wallace, *Buddhism & Science: Breaking New Ground* (New York: Columbia University Press, 2003), 253.

33   *like letters which are not opened* Gail Bixler-Thomas, "Understanding Dreams: Perspectives from the Ancients Through Modern Times," November 1998, accessed March 29, 2012, http://www.erhsgraphics.com/Dreaming.html.

33   *but also for an entire community, and were used* Robert Moss, *Dreamways of the Iroquois: Honoring the Secret Wishes of the Soul* (Rochester, VT: Destiny Books, 2005).

34   *looked on as being evil and sinful* Christopher Dewdney, *Acquainted with the Night: Excursions Through the World After Dark* (New York: Bloomsbury, 2004), 167.

34   *dreams were insubstantial* Chrysostom John and Catharine P. Roth, *On Wealth and Poverty* (Crestwood, NY: St. Vladimir's Seminary, 1984), 12.

34   *possessed no real value* Raymond L. Lee, "Forgotten Fantasies," *Dreaming* 20 (2010): 291.

34   *they were secular* Ibid., 291–93.

36   *visions as "just dreams"* Edain McCoy, *Astral Projection for Beginners: Learn Several Techniques to Gain a Broad Awareness of Other Realms of Existence* (St. Paul, MN: Llewellyn Publications, 1999).

CHAPTER 4: *The REM Stage*

44   *studying his sleeping patterns* Chip Brown, "The Stubborn Scientist Who Unraveled a Mystery of the Night," *Smithsonian Magazine,* October 2003.

44   *his brain were wide awake* William Dement and Nathaniel Kleitman, "The Relation of Eye Movements During Sleep to Dream Activity: An Objective Method for the Study of Dreaming," *Journal of Experimental Psychology* 53 (1957): 339–46.

44 *I was absolutely finished* Tony Crisp, "Eugene Aserinsky," *Dreamhawk*, 2011, http://dreamhawk.com/interesting-people/eugene-aserinsky/.

45 *during a specific time within sleep* DeGuzman and Morton, "REM Sleep."

45 *essentially similar brain states* Paul R. Martin, *Counting Sheep: The Science and Pleasures of Sleep and Dreams* (New York: Thomas Dunne Books/St. Martin's Press, 2004).

45 *active agents in creating our experience* R. Llinás and D. Paré, "Of Dreaming and Wakefuless," *Neuroscience* 44 (1991): 521–35.

48 *strengthening your immune system* Hartmut Schulz, "Rethinking Sleep Analysis," *Journal of Clinical Sleep Medicine* 2008, 4 (2): 99–103. http://www.ncbi.nlm.nih.gov/pmc/articles/PMC2335403/.

48 *the very seat of dreams* "What Happens When You Sleep," National Sleep Foundation, http://www.sleepfoundation.org/article/how-sleep-works/what-happens-when-you-sleep.

CHAPTER 5: *The Power of Intention*

52 *Bannister's record with 3:58* Bruce Lowitt, "Bannister Stuns World With 4-Minute Mile," *Tampa Bay Times* (St. Petersburg, FL), December 17, 1999.

52 *at a whopping 3:43* "El Guerrouj Hicham Biography," Iaaf.org (International Association of Athletics Federations), http://www.iaaf.org/athletes/biographies/letter=e/athcode=9824/index.html.

53 *associated with the skeletal muscles* "Electromyograph," definition 1, The Free Dictionary by Farlex, 2009, from *The American Heritage Dictionary of the English Language,* http://www.thefreedictionary.com/electromyograph.

54 *the same mental instructions as action* Lynne McTaggart, *The Intention Experiment: Using Your Thoughts to Change Your Life and the World* (New York: Free Press, 2007).

54 *a thought and a real-life event* R. M. Suinn, "Imagery Rehearsal Applications in Performance Enhancement," *Behavioral Therapist* 8 (1985): 155–59.

54 *significantly increase muscle strength* Philip Cohen, "Mental Gymnastics Increase Bicep Strength," *New Scientist,* November 21, 2001, http://www.newscientist.com/article/dn1591-mental-gymnastics-increase-bicep-strength.html.

CHAPTER 6: *Remembering Your Dreams*

64 *or whether we're remembering dreams* Cristina Marzano, Michele Ferrara, Federica Mauro, Fabio Moroni, Maurizio Gorgoni, Daniela Tempesta, Carlo Cipolli, and Luigi De Gennaro. "Recalling and Forgetting Dreams: Theta and Alpha Oscillations During Sleep Predict Subsequent Dream Recall," *The Journal of Neuroscience* 31 (2011).

64 *conflict the dream might be hinting at* Marilyn Schlitz and Frank Pascoe. "The Achuar Dream Practices," Mystic Mountain Center for Healing Arts, http://www.mystical company.com/Achuar.php.

66   *main factors in sleep loss* "TV Before Bed Causes Chronic Health Problems, Study Claims," *The Telegraph*, June 9, 2009, http://www.telegraph.co.uk/culture/tvand radio/5483296/TV-before-bed-causes-chronic-health-problems-study-claims.html.

67   *extending the stage of deep sleep* I. Feinberg, R. Jones, J. M. Walker, C. Cavness, and J. March, "Effects of High Dosage Delta-9-tetrahydrocannabinol on Sleep Patterns in Man," *Clinical Pharmacology and Therapeutics* 17 (1975): 458–66.

69   *report other vivid nocturnal experiences* D. Watson, "To Dream, Perchance to Remember: Individual Differences in Dream Recall," *Personality and Individual Differences* 34 (2003): 1271–86.

CHAPTER 7: *Keeping a Dream Journal*

72   *90 percent is lost* Robert J. Hoss, "Questions about Dream "Language," DreamScience, http://dreamscience.org/idx_faq.htm.

74   *one of his most useful techniques* C. M. Den Blanken, and E. J. Meijer, "An Historical View of Dreams and the Ways to Direct Them: Practical Observations by Marie-Jean-Leon Lecoq, le Marquis d'Hervey-Saint-Denys," Spiritwatch, http://spiritwatch.ca/lucidity06.html.

77   *a question we haven't learned to ask* "Memorable Quotes for 'The X-Files' Paper Hearts (1996)," IMDb, accessed September 2, 2011, http://www.imdb.com/title/tt0751175/quotes.

78   *the more the dreamer can learn* David Fontana, *Teach Yourself to Dream: A Practical Guide to Unleashing the Power of the Subconscious Mind* (San Francisco: Chronicle Books, 1997).

80   *from yellow to green to red* Charles Darwin to John Stevens Henslow, May 18, 1832, Rio de Janeiro, http://www.darwinproject.ac.uk/entry-171.

CHAPTER 9: *Becoming Lucid*

100   *Aldrin used the phrase "magnificent desolation"* "One Small Step." Apollo 11 Lunar Surface Journal, accessed February 22, 2012, http://www.hq.nasa.gov/alsj/a11/a11.step.html.

100   *tend to happen in this way* Stephen LaBerge and Howard Rheingold, *Exploring the World of Lucid Dreaming* (New York: Ballantine Books, 1991).

102   *your mind is primed for dreaming* Mark Stibich, "The Stages of Sleep," About.com Longevity, accessed January 24, 2009, http://longevity.about.com/od/sleep/a/sleep_stages.htm.

107   *that's a long one for me* Heidi Blake, "Apollo 11 Moon Landing: Top Quotes from the Mission That Put Man on the Moon," *The Telegraph*, July 20, 2009, http://www.telegraph.co.uk/science/space/5843299/Apollo-11-moon-landing-top-quotes-from-the-mission-that-put-man-on-the-moon.html.

CHAPTER 10: *Staying Lucid*

114 *closely related with visual information* Stephen LaBerge, "Prolonging Lucid Dreams," *NightLight* 7 (1995).

114 *dream world to the waking world* LaBerge and Rheingold, "Chapter 6: Principles and Practice of Lucid Dreaming," *Exploring the World of Lucid Dreaming.*

115 *Be in the world, but not of it* John 17:14–15, *Holy Bible*, English Standard Version (Wheaton, IL: Crossway Bibles, 2001).

CHAPTER 11: *Transportation*

136 *simply appear out of the blackness* Martin, *Counting Sheep*, 216.

139 *bring you into a scene from another era* Moss, *Dreamgates*, 119.

CHAPTER 12: *Creation*

141 *and art from an early pueblo society* Benjamin Alfred Wetherill and Maurine S. Fletcher, *The Wetherills of the Mesa Verde: Autobiography of Benjamin Alfred Wetherill* (Lincoln: University of Nebraska Press, 1987).

143 *clutter like a determined chambermaid* George Dvorsky, "Managing Your 50,000 Daily Thoughts," *Sentient Developments* (blog), March 19, 2007, http://www.sentient developments.com/2007/03/managing-your-50000-daily-thoughts.html.

CHAPTER 13: *The Natives*

161 *the characters in their dreams felt something* David Kahn and Allan Hobson, "Theory of Mind in Dreaming: Awareness of Feelings and Thoughts of Others in Dreams," *Dreaming* 15 (2005): 48–57.

163 *things which I had not consciously thought* C. G. Jung, *Memories, Dreams, Reflections* (New York: Pantheon Books, 1963).

165 *paid for this deception with his life* George Parker Winship, ed. and trans., *The Journey of Coronado, 1540–1542, from the City of Mexico to the Grand Canyon of the Colorado and the Buffalo Plains of Texas, Kansas, and Nebraska, as Told by Himself and His Followers* (New York: A. S. Barnes & Co, 1904), 142–215.

CHAPTER 15: *Defusing Nightmares*

183 *one or more nightmares a month* Richard C. Wilkerson, "Common Questions About Nightmares," International Association for the Study of Dreams, http://www.asdreams .org/nightma.htm.

183 *about two nightmares per month were reported* M. Schredl and D. Erlacher, "Lucid Dreaming Frequency and Personality," *Personality and Individual Differences* 37 (2004): 1463–73.

184 *a separate study of Chinese students* Calvin Kai-Ching Yu, "Dream Intensity Inventory and Chinese People's Dream Experience Frequencies," *Dreaming* 18 (2008): 94–111.

186 *they are missing parts of ourselves* Robert Waggoner, *Lucid Dreaming: Gateway to the Inner Self* (Needham, MA: Moment Point Press, 2009), 18.

186 *becoming whole and balanced people* Ruth Snowden, *Jung: The Key Ideas* (Blacklick, OH: McGraw-Hill, 2010), 54.

187 *I rode on the back of that shark* LaBerge and Rheingold, *Exploring the World of Lucid Dreaming*, 251–52.

189 *when we confront a nightmare, we conquer it* Ibid., 236.

191 *often make the nightmarish figure stronger* Ibid.

CHAPTER 16: *Healing and Wholeness*

195 *you are looking for a dream* Lewis Richard Farnell, Chapter 10, *Greek Hero Cults and Ideas of Immortality: The Gifford Lectures Delivered in the University of St. Andrews in the Year 1920* (Oxford: Clarendon Press, 1921), 234–79.

196 *reported to have vanished with the help of dreams* Rosemary E. Guiley, "The Healing Power of Dreams," Visionary Living with Rosemary Ellen Guiley, http://www.visionary living.com/articles/healingdreams.php.

196 *writes neuroscientist Candace Pert* Candace B. Pert, *Molecules of Emotion: Why You Feel the Way You Feel* (New York: Scribner, 1997).

197 *the main goal of all therapy is integration* Colin Wilson, *New Pathways in Psychology: Maslow and the Post-Freudian Revolution* (London: Victor Gollancz, 1973).

197 *Psychologists call this dissociation* Paul F. Dell and John A. O'Neil. *Dissociation and the Dissociative Disorders: DSM-V and Beyond* (New York: Routledge, 2009), xix–xxi.

198 *healing means "to make whole"* Douglas Harper, ed. "Heal," Online Etymology Dictionary, 2001, http://www.etymonline.com/index.php?term=heal.

201 *and reducing some side effects of chemotherapy* "Imagery," American Cancer Society, http://www.cancer.org/treatment/treatmentsandsideeffects/complementaryandalternative medicine/mindbodyandspirit/imagery.

201 *allergies, diabetes, heart disease, and carpal tunnel syndrome* "Medical Conditions," Academy for Guided Imagery, http://acadgi.com/researchfindings/medicalconditions/ index.html.

CHAPTER 17: *Dream Incubation*

206 *she will do very well as a fisherman's daughter* Anna Bonus Kingsford and Edward Maitland, *Dreams and Dream-Stories* (London: George Redway, 1888).

207   *in hopes of receiving divine advice about their troubles* Moss, *Secret History of Dreaming,* 11–12.

208   *and ropes under the subject's skin* Henri F. Ellenberger, *The Discovery of the Unconscious: The History and Evolution of Dynamic Psychiatry* (New York: Basic Books, 1970), 8.

208   *and the reports were confirmed* Deirdre Barrett, "The 'Committee of Sleep': A Study of Dream Incubation for Problem Solving," *Dreaming* 3 (1993).

215   *would enlist the help of a dream priest* Moss, *Secret History of Dreaming,* 11–12.

CHAPTER 18: *WILD*

217   *a spontaneous realization* LaBerge and Rheingold, *Exploring the World of Lucid Dreaming.*

218   *or WILD for short* Richard R. Bootzin, John F. Kihlstrom, Daniel L. Schacter, and Stephen LaBerge, "Lucid Dreaming: Psychophysiological Studies of Consciousness during REM Sleep," *Sleep and Cognition* (Washington, DC: American Psychological Association, 1990), 109–26.

220   *the optimal state for creativity* N. V. Zhilkina, "The Extreme Component in Idea Generation," in Russian, *Analytical Culturology* 2 (2006).

220   *the cusp between sleeping and waking* Moss, *Secret History of Dreaming,* 139.

222   *which they can enter any time they please* Robert Moss, *Active Dreaming: Journeying Beyond Self-Limitation to a Life of Wild Freedom* (Novato, CA: New World Library, 2011).

222   *relativity whirling around in his head* Moss, *Secret History of Dreaming.*

222   *solar system with the sun and planets* Ibid.

222   *images will come," says Moss* Robert Moss, "Spend More Time in the Twilight Zone," *Timeless Spirit Magazine,* 2002, accessed October 22, 2011, http://www.timeless spirit.com/MAR04/robert.shtml.

224   *it cannot move while you dream* R. Lydic, "The Motor Atonia of REM Sleep: a Critical Topics Forum," *Sleep* 2008. 31:1471–72.

224   *occurs during non-REM sleep* Jenifer Swanson, ed. "Sleepwalking," in *Sleep Disorders Sourcebook* (Detroit: Omnigraphics, 1999), 249–54, 351–52.

224   *a state of attentive relaxation* LaBerge and Rheingold, *Exploring the World of Lucid Dreaming,* 139.

CHAPTER 19: *Know Thyself*

233   *discover the treasure of their true selves* Carol L. Pearson, ThinkExist.com, http://thinkexist.com/quotation/heroes_take_journeys-confront_dragons-and/201756.html.

234 *unconscious activities of the mind* Ernest Hartmann, *Dreams and Nightmares: The Origin and Meaning of Dreams* (Cambridge, MA: Perseus, 2001), 173.

235 *become whole, believed Jung* Snowden, *Jung: The Key Ideas*, 54.

238 *change his awareness of himself* Abraham Maslow, "Maslow Quotes," *Abraham Maslow: Father of Modern Management,* 2005, http://www.abraham-maslow.com/m_ motivation/Maslow_Quotes.asp.

CHAPTER 20: *Waking vs. Dreaming*

244 *able to have peak experiences daily* Abraham H. Maslow, *Toward a Psychology of Being* (Princeton, NJ: Van Nostrand, 1968).

246 *our experiences are 'real' and external to our own mind* Tenzin Wangyal and Mark Dahlby. *The Tibetan Yogas of Dream and Sleep* (Ithaca, NY: Snow Lion Publications, 1998), 33.

248 *as a particle behaves or like a wave* Brian Greene, *The Elegant Universe: Superstrings, Hidden Dimensions, and the Quest for the Ultimate Theory* (New York: W.W. Norton, 1999), 98.

248 *tiny charged particles floating around* Ibid., 97–279.

250 *in the 25 to 30 Hz range–gamma waves!* John Geirland, "Buddha on the Brain," *Wired 14.02,* February 2006, http://www.wired.com/wired/archive/14.02/dalai.html.

250 *higher than the Dalai Lama's best meditators* Ursula Voss, PhD, Romain Holzmann, Dr. Inka Tuin, MD, and Allan Hobson, MD, "Lucid Dreaming: A State of Consciousness with Features of Both Waking and Non-Lucid Dreaming." *Sleep* 32.9 (2009), 1191–1200.

CHAPTER 21: *A Future Vision*

253 *some 150,000 years ago* Dennis O'Neil, "Early Modern Homo sapiens," *Evolution of Modern Humans: A Survey of the Biological and Cultural Evolution of Archaic and Modern Homo sapiens,* December 24, 2011, accessed March 12, 2012, http://anthro.palomar.edu/ homo2/mod_homo_4.htm.

253 *Latin for "man wise wise"* Douglas Harper, ed. "Homo Sapiens." Online Etymology Dictionary. 2001, http://www.etymonline.com/index.php?term=homo+sapiens.

254 *"he who knows he knows"* Michael J. Mahoney, *Human Change Processes: The Scientific Foundations of Psychotherapy* (New York: Basic Books, 1991), 442.

258 *at last you create what you will* Stephen Winsten, G.B.S. 90: *Aspects of Bernard Shaw's Life and Work* (New York: Dodd, Mead & Co., 1946), 63.

ACKNOWLEDGMENTS

We'd like to give a lotta love and gratitude to the people who helped make this book happen. First off, thanks to our parents for dreaming us into existence. To all our wonderful Kickstarter backers, who took a leap of faith with their checkbooks. Without them this book would still be an idea. Thanks to the team at Kickstarter, specifically Yancey Strickler and Kendel Ratley, for helping bring our project to life. Lots of gratitude to Bruce Tracy at Workman for guiding us with wit, wisdom, and the occasional pinch of cheekiness. Our lovely agent, Andrea Somberg, for finding us in a sea of New York writers—we're grateful for your unlimited patience and confidence. Our buddies, Kyle O'Tain and Camille DeMere, for reading our early drafts and telling us when the mark had been missed, and to our other readers Terry Soloway, Brian Miller, and Edye Weissler. To Mallory Grigg, who threw us a life jacket when we were over our heads in InDesign. Rebecca Storch and Lauren Pennline for stamping, shipping, and supporting us throughout. And thanks to the talented Krasimir Galabov for creating a beautiful digital laboratory for us.

Jared: Much thanks to my brothers, Austin and Simon, for hawking early copies of this book to their classmates. Lots of thanks to my cousin, Michael, for introducing me to lucid dreaming in the first place. To all my family, friends, and loved ones, thanks for their infinite support on this adventure.

Dylan: Thanks to Linda Dawson for letting me blab about this book for two years, and for her always present love and support. Thanks to Emma Tuccillo for hand-binding a two-hundred-and-fifty-page book and for all her enthusiasm. To Sean Tuccillo for being a sounding board, and for calling me when Kickstarter was exploding. And to all my family and friends.

Thomas: To you—the bold, the courageous, the ones ready and willing to awaken the dreamer. Together, we will remember ourselves to be infinite.

Lastly, thanks to all the authors, researchers, and dreamers who came before us. We are only continuing along a path that has already been pioneered.

ABOUT THE AUTHORS

Thomas Peisel, Jared Zeizel, and Dylan Tuccillo are award-winning writers and filmmakers, each with his own story. Thomas began his exploits in the dream world as a teenager. After becoming lucid spontaneously, he began immersing himself in books, articles, and anything he could find that might help him understand this unique experience. Since then, he has flown above the clouds with geese, run through the woods as a wolf, created a galaxy, and met with various teachers in his dreams. His greatest advice was given to him by a seven-foot-tall Abraham Lincoln. Jared also learned about lucid dreaming during his teenage years. He's bathed in the sunlight while flying, battled giant robot ninjas, conversed with the darker aspects of himself, and practiced controlling energy. He looks at lucid dreaming as a chance to step through the mirror of dreaming, an opportunity to push the veil of our reality aside and glimpse at the nature of the universe. He also likes hanging out with baby tiger cubs. Dylan was introduced to lucid dreaming by Thomas after the two met at college. He gawked at this amazing ability and soon found himself flying over the ocean, talking with guides, and exploring Mexican villages. The three started thinking about *A Field Guide to Lucid Dreaming* in late 2010. "If only the rest of the world could wake up in their dreams!" they thought. All three authors live in Manhattan. Their website is dreamlabs.io.